MIKE JOHNSON

FROM SPECTATOR TO
TRUE
WORSHIPPER

WESTBOW
PRESS®
A DIVISION OF THOMAS NELSON
& ZONDERVAN

WestBow Press books may be ordered through booksellers or by contacting:

WestBow Press
A Division of Thomas Nelson & Zondervan
1663 Liberty Drive
Bloomington, IN 47403
www.westbowpress.com
844-714-3454

Scripture quotations are taken from the New King James Version. Copyright © 1982 by Thomas Nelson, Inc. Used by permission. All rights reserved.

Cover art by Emmanuel Ahenkan
Author photo by Karen Kodish Photography

ISBN: 979-8-3850-1882-6 (sc)
ISBN: 979-8-3850-1883-3 (e)

Library of Congress Control Number: 2024902927

Print information available on the last page.

WestBow Press rev. date: 03/04/2025

Contents

Chapter 1

My Journey to Becoming a Worshipper

My name is Mike, and I am a practising worshipper. That's because, for most of my life, I have been conditioned to be a spectator. When I am in church, I sit, and others do things for me. Someone collects my offering, someone prays for me, someone (or a group) sings to me, and someone preaches to me and tells me when to say, "Amen." My question is, if someone does it for me, or tells me when and how to say it, when do I exercise my choice to worship God in the way He inspires? Am I worshipping God as led by His Spirit or going through a list of things that others have planned for me? This lack of engagement is what leads to boredom, fatigue, and eventually, a falling away from the church community. The feeling of exclusion is an open door for dissatisfaction and apathy, which makes it easier to slip away.

I am sure it is not intentional, but training in spectatorship begins at an early age with children's stories. We have matured into adulthood, and we are still sitting down and waiting for a story (sermon) from the preacher. All this stems from generations of people going to church to worship instead of worshipping at home and then coming together to share at church. This is assuming that the church worship experience allows for expressions of worship by the congregants through testimonies and other acceptable forms of worship.

As I discovered the biblical principles of worship, I had to question what I had been doing, or not, and then start to incorporate these principles into my home worship first. Then I had to cope with the frustration of wanting to do the same in a congregational setting that does not cater for it regularly. A close examination of biblical and contemporary worship patterns reveals a concerning difference that calls for urgent review as we strive to harmonise with the worship of heaven.

Worship is at the root of the struggle that we are a part of — this controversy between Satan and Christ. The work of the devil is to muddy the waters by introducing complications and unnecessary elements into worship services that will cause bemusement and uncertainty about what God expects. For these reasons, now is the time for individuals to connect with God's principles of worship and to implement them in the home, as a matter of priority. The COVID-19 pandemic closed churches for a while but consider if Christ had come during that period and we had to give an account of our worship experience. Would you be saying, "I wanted to, but the government said that I couldn't attend church, and my pastor was on furlough"? Really?

Jesus will not be conducting a roll call of denominations or churches when He comes again, but we will be accountable as individuals, and so we need to wean ourselves off looking to others to plan occasions for us and end up extending our days as spectators. We need to "seek first His righteousness," His way of doing the things that are pleasing in His sight. God has done something marvellous in giving us this ability to worship Him, which is a preview of eternity. There are very few church-related activities and practices that will last forever, which highlights the importance of paying close attention to those that will, such as the Sabbath, worship, and music. "'For as the new heavens and the new earth which I will make shall remain before Me,' says the Lord, 'So shall your descendants and your name remain, and it shall come to pass that from one New Moon to another, and from one Sabbath to another, all flesh shall come to worship before Me,' says the Lord" (Isaiah 66:22–23). If your gift is for music, yours is an eternal ministry, and in all the discussions and controversy over music, let that thought frame your purpose and how you apply this gift.

The genesis of my journey to becoming a worshipper began with a couple of experiences that caused me to evaluate what I had (or had not) been doing, and it occurred in two church services from differing traditions—Seventh-day Adventist and Catholic. There is a lesson in that statement because it shows that God has people in every faith tradition who are worshipping Him with all the knowledge they possess, and He accepts them, and if God accepts them, who am I to demonise them? Just because someone believes differently does not mean they have no hope. On the first occasion, I was at a music conference at the Riverside Seventh-day Adventist Church in Nashville, Tennessee, in 2008. At that event, the good and the great of Adventist musicians and worship leaders were present, and the music was rich and powerful. I found myself wanting to sing, but I could not because I had a lump in my throat. The phrase, "Angels had to fold their wings" from the hymn "Holy, Holy Is What the Angels Sing" came to mind. It was as if the Lord was saying to me, "Keep quiet, watch, and learn." I had not experienced anything like that before.

The second time was in a Catholic church (Saint Sabina) in Chicago, and it began when I was on a tour of the Washington DC area with a gospel group that I was managing. As part of the tour, we received an invitation to sing at the Sunday service at Howard University where Father Michael Pfleger was the guest speaker. After the service, he invited the group to come and sing at his church in Chicago the following February as part of Black History Month. Saint Sabina is a majority Black church, and that weekend, he had Cornel

West and Michael Eric Dyson as part of the proceedings. The penny dropped for me in the Sunday morning worship service when there was an opportunity for worshippers to leave their seats and express their worship. It was a thing of beauty, and as I witnessed them, I heard myself say, "Mike, you don't know how to worship." It was the Samaritan woman and Jesus all over again. I had been doing things one way for all these years, but now the Lord was revealing the truth to me.

Looking back on these experiences taught me that God was schooling me for the time when I would serve as music director at the regional office of my church; He was encouraging me to make worship my focus. My goal was to work with all those engaged in the weekly worship services to show how pastors, musicians, singers, and members can unite to enhance the worship experience and assist members in transitioning from spectators to true worshippers.

In this book, you will find biblical principles of worship that will help you to connect with God for your own experiences. It is not a prescription to follow because no one person or committee can prescribe worship formats, although many have tried, and we are still "slaves" to those attempts. Look at how God gives us brand-new mercies and blessings every day, yet we go through the same ritual every week. That makes no sense. Worship is an expression of who God is and what He has done for you, and it should be a way of life and not just a weekly activity. Start at home so that experiences (testimonies) will accompany you to church each week. You will come to see that "true worshippers"—the ones God is looking for—are those inspired by the Holy Spirit, worshipping from the heart, and producing worship that is acceptable to God. Unacceptable worship is when you are in a place of worship, but your heart, or your mind, is far away. It is also when you are in a place of worship, but you are not on good terms with a fellow worshipper—such worship is in vain, says the Lord.

Chapter 2

There Was War
in Heaven

So, how did this struggle, the battle over worship, begin? Although we have never been to heaven, we think of it in idyllic terms, and we describe moments of happiness and success as "heavenly." It seems inconceivable, therefore, that this could happen, but it's true: there was war in heaven: "And war broke out in heaven; Michael (another name for Jesus) and his angels fought with the dragon; and the dragon and his angels fought, but they did not prevail, nor was a place found for them in heaven any longer. So, the great dragon was cast out, that serpent of old, called the Devil and Satan, who deceives the whole world; he was cast to the earth, and his angels were cast out with him" (Revelation 12:7–9).

I must confess that when I first read about this war as a young adult, I pictured a physical scenario with death on each side. That is because: "When I was a child, I thought as a child" (1 Corinthians 13:11). But I know better now, because Lucifer and the angels he deceived participated in a struggle—not to the death or with the shedding of blood but over sovereignty and worship. The original director of music began to sow seeds of discord and doubt in heaven, resulting in his expulsion from heaven, along with a third of the angelic hosts. Listen to the warning that accompanied their expulsion: "Therefore rejoice, O heavens, and you who dwell in them! Woe to the inhabitants of the earth and the sea! For the devil has come down to you, having great wrath, because he knows that he has a short time" (Revelation 12:12). Notice how the inhabitants of the heavens (other worlds) can rejoice because they did not succumb to the deceit and schemes of the devil. On the other hand, we are issued with a "Woe." We need to watch out for the schemes and plans of the arch-deceiver, counterfeiter, "Father of lies", and originator of sin because he is on a mission to take as many as possible with him on his journey to destruction: "For by your sorcery all the nations were deceived" (Revelation 18:23). The apostle Peter echoes the call for watchfulness when he says: "Be sober, be vigilant; because your adversary the devil walks about like a roaring lion, seeking whom he may devour" (1 Peter 5:8). Satan's go-to method is the use of misinformation, spreading lies and rumours about Christ while hiding his true motive of jealousy—wanting what belongs to Christ and risking his own life and the lives of others to get it.

The Controversy

We know there was contention between Lucifer and Christ, but what would cause such a toxic atmosphere in heaven? One thing that we do know is that, from the day God created Lucifer, he was perfect. The Bible puts it this way: "You were perfect in your ways from the day you were created, until iniquity was found in you" (Ezekiel 28:15). God did not create evil, and He did not create sin. To fully understand Lucifer's iniquity, we need to take a step back and look at the position he occupied in heaven, specifically in his service to God. In today's terminology, he would be the Chief of Staff. In the government of heaven, the throne (a key word in the context of our subject) was at the centre of heaven's administration.

6

God sits on the throne, and on either side of the throne are two "covering cherubs" facing each other, and their wings touched as they cover the throne.

There is never a moment in heaven when worship is not being offered to God or Jesus. As the chief angel before his fall and heaven's music director, this truth was not lost on Lucifer. Consider this example: "The four living creatures, each having six wings, were full of eyes around and within. And they do not rest day or night, saying: 'Holy, holy, holy, Lord God Almighty, Who was and is and is to come!'" (Revelation 4:8).

Lucifer was created with unparalleled beauty, immense power, and extraordinary abilities, lacking nothing. Yet, despite his perfection, he grew discontent. As he observed the unceasing honour and glorification of God, a dangerous thought began to stir within him—a desire for the worship that belonged to God alone.

Battle of the Thrones

The war in heaven was a battle of thrones. (Revelation 4:10; 7:9–12) and others speak of worship belonging to the One who "sits on the throne." We find the script for our epic struggle in the book of Isaiah: "In the year that King Uzziah died, I saw the Lord sitting on a throne, high and lifted up, and the train of His robe filled the temple" (Isaiah 6:1). Now, contrast Satan's intention: "For you have said in your heart: 'I will ascend into heaven; I will exalt my throne above the stars of God'" (Isaiah 14:13). He goes further to say, "I will ascend above the heights of the clouds, I will be like the Most-High" (Isaiah 14:14). Notice the conflict in the positioning of the thrones. The Lord's throne was "high and lifted up," yet Satan says he—a created being—will exalt his throne "above the Most-High." Not only does he want what belongs to God, he wants to be God, and he made no secret of it.

Satan's desire for worship was also evident during his temptation of Christ in the wilderness. He claimed ownership of the world but was prepared to give it up, saying, "If you will worship before me, all will be yours" (Luke 4:7). We see another depiction of it in the three angels' messages of (Revelation 14:6–10). The first and third messages are specific.

First Angel—Encouragement to Worship the Creator:

"Worship Him who made heaven and earth, the sea and springs of water" (Revelation 14:7). The apostle John begins his gospel with a confirmation of the status of Jesus Christ. He writes, "In the beginning was the Word [Jesus], and the Word was with God, and the Word was God. He was in the beginning with God. All things were made through Him, and without Him, nothing was made that was made. In Him was life, and the life was the light of men" (John 1:1–4). This is clear. Jesus, God the Son, is the Creator of the world, and if your worship is not to Him, it is in vain. To help you make the right choices, the enabling Holy Spirit is within all of us, and His effectiveness is dependent on your willingness to give Him control.

Third Angel—Warning against Worshipping Satan:

"If anyone worships the beast and his image ... he himself shall also drink of the wine of the wrath of God" (Revelation 14:9–10). Satan has never created anything apart from destruction and lies; he is the "father of lies." His task in life is to kill, steal, and destroy. He knows he has a brief time before he meets his judgement and destruction, and he plans to take others with him to the fires of hell, which are prepared for the devil and his angels. Matthew 25 reveals two distinct places for the saved and the lost: "Then He will also say to those on the left hand, 'Depart from Me, you cursed, into the everlasting fire [its effects] prepared for the devil and his angels'" (Matthew 25:41). If your allegiance is to him, that is where you will end up. But please notice the specified occupants— "the devil and his angels." Our future residence is somewhere completely different: "Come, you blessed of My Father, inherit the kingdom prepared for you from the foundation of the world" (Matthew 25:34). You do not have to actively choose to follow the devil, but if you reject or ignore Christ, you end up on the other side.

The "Beast" is a prophetic term for a religious or political force that will attempt to change laws and prerogatives that belong to God. This power originates from the Antichrist, who, along with his agents, will enforce these changes. In the context of this book, I am not speaking about individuals but about institutions and the basis on which they operate. I refer you to my earlier statement that there are individuals in every tradition who are worshipping God to all that they know. The question for us is who will we worship, and how are we to worship? because God is looking for "true worshippers." In the old days, bank tellers would hold up banknotes to the sun to confirm authenticity, but will your worship pass the test when held up before the Lord?

In the Christian tradition, there are two dominant days of worship: Saturday, as outlined in Scripture, and Sunday. At the time of writing, worshippers are free to worship on the day of their choice, but a time is coming when one day will be enforceable as the only day of worship, and there will be negative consequences for those who go against this law; their livelihood will be threatened, and a choice will have to be made—protect myself and my family and go against what I've known and believed all my life, or do I stand on the side of Christ and risk everything? For those who are determined to stand for Christ, even to the point of death, Christ has a promise: "For whoever desires to save his life will lose it, but whoever loses his life for My sake will find it" (Matthew 16:25).

Chapter 3

Called to Worship

When God sent His representatives, Moses, and Aaron, to Pharaoh, it was with the message to "Let My people go, that they may serve, or worship Me" (Exodus 8:1). Throughout the wilderness years, the people murmured and longed for the sights and tastes of Egypt. So much so that when Moses was gone for a long time, they coerced Aaron to "make us gods" (Exodus 32:1). Aaron capitulated and made the golden calf, one of the Egyptian gods to which they had become accustomed; the result was that three thousand people lost their lives that day (Exodus 32:28). Contrast the people's request to "make us gods" with David's assertion: "Know that the Lord, He is God; it is He who has made us, and not we ourselves" (Psalm 100:3). The danger with making gods is that you must protect them when it should be the other way round. Anything you devote more time or resources to, above God, is a god, and we have all fallen into that trap. The material used for this golden idol was part of the excess that they plundered from their Egyptian masters, and they were to wear it until the required time.

The call to worship is still applicable today because, for generations, God's people have been following rigid forms of liturgy and have become spectators in the house of worship. We have become reliant on those who stand before us, and when the opportunity comes for the expression of worship, paralysis grips part of the congregation because of their lack of experience in sharing their testimonies or because they have no testimony. We are watching worship, even though worship is a sacred act that we offer to God. As soon as children can speak, parents should teach them how to express their worship in their unique ways: "'Do You hear what these are saying?' And Jesus said to them, 'Yes. Have you never read, "Out of the mouth of babes and nursing infants You have perfected praise"?'" (Matthew 21:16). In this way, we are training them in the act of testifying.

Let My People Go

In Exodus 3, we read of the call of Moses and his commissioning by God to deliver His people from oppression in Egypt. God cites the reasons for acting as, "I have surely seen the oppression of My people who are in Egypt, and have heard their cry because of their taskmasters, for I know their sorrows. So, I have come down to deliver them out of the hand of the Egyptians, and to bring them up from that land to a good and large land, to a land flowing with milk and honey … Now therefore, behold, the cry of the children of Israel has come to Me, and I have also seen the oppression with which the Egyptians oppress them. Come now, therefore, and I will send you to Pharaoh that you may bring My people, the children of Israel, out of Egypt" (Exodus 3:7–10). What a beautiful thought that, when it comes to our deliverance, the Godhead takes it personally. God came down to rescue His people from the Egyptians. God also made an intervention when He came down to speak with Cain to try and avert the deadly course he was on. The model prayer of Matthew 6:13 teaches us to pray, "Lead us not into temptation." In other words, do not allow me to fall into temptation. Jesus also came down to die on Calvary's cross.

Lesson #1 from this exchange is that God sees and knows everything, and when He sees that we are heading towards danger, temptation, or sin, His love for us causes Him to intervene. In Exodus 3:3–5, He noticed that Moses was about to head towards the burning bush for a closer look, but because that would be injurious to him, God called out to him. After an exchange in which Moses tried to disqualify himself for a variety of reasons, I can imagine God stopping the conversation by saying, "Moses, stop whining for a moment and listen. If I call you, I will equip you." That is because God knows all our weaknesses and faults, and despite this, He is still willing to call us into service. This should fill us with the confidence that, with God on our side, we have no need to worry.

I want to consider the difference between the reason God gave to Moses for the deliverance of His people (oppression) and the specific message that Moses was to give to Pharaoh (worship). The Pharaohs are gods, as well as serving as links between the people and the various gods they worshipped. I contend that God was sending a direct message (DM) in a head-to-head challenge to Pharaoh (true God to substitute-god) to say, "Let My people go so they can worship Me." Pharaoh regarded the people as his possession, but I hear an emphasis on "My" and "Me" in God's message to Pharaoh. I am also asking myself, "Is worship the way to escape from our physical struggles?" "Seek first the kingdom of God and His righteousness, and all these things will be added to you" (Matthew 6:33). When the nation of Judah was under siege and outnumbered, they prioritised worship, and God then fought on their behalf (2 Chronicles 20:21–24).

The story of the Exodus is fundamentally about worship, beginning with the leaders. The Lord anticipated that Pharaoh would demand a miracle from Moses and Aaron to prove their legitimacy. Following God's instructions, Aaron threw his staff to the ground, and it became a serpent. In response, Pharaoh summoned his team, who also threw their staffs to the ground, and they turned into serpents. However, Aaron's serpent devoured all the others (Exodus 7:8-12).

The Exodus is also a shadow of what we are going through today because we are under the oppression of sin, terrorised by Satan, who is seeking to destroy us through pain and death. But the Lord looked ahead in time and made provisions for our release through the death of Jesus Christ on the cross. We must reject the customs and practices of society, including those that have crept into the church, and instead seek to do things that will glorify God.

The other worship lesson from the Exodus is that of the ten plagues because each one was a direct challenge to an Egyptian god, and in these examples, the Lord was establishing His supremacy in the eyes of the rulers and the people. Modern warfare speaks of "precision bombing" to avoid collateral damage, but that is nothing new because while the plagues destroyed everything in the fields—humans and animals—they did not touch God's people in the enclave of Goshen (Exodus 9:22–26). The psalmist David puts it this way: "He who dwells in the secret place of the Most-High shall abide under the shadow (protection) of the Almighty. I will say of the Lord, 'He is my refuge and my fortress; My God, in Him I will trust.' Surely, He shall deliver you from the snare of the fowler and from the perilous pestilence. He shall cover you with His feathers, and under His wings you shall take refuge; His truth shall be your shield and buckler. You shall not be afraid of the terror by night, nor of the arrow that flies by day, nor of the pestilence that walks in darkness, nor of the destruction that wastes at noonday. A thousand may fall at your side, and ten thousand at your right hand; but it shall not come near you" (Psalm 91:1–7).

That same level of protection and deliverance is also available to us today. One by one, God was defeating all other gods before Him. The Hebrew people had become familiar with these gods and heathen worship, so the Lord emphasised the futility of worshipping other gods by embedding a warning in the Ten Commandments (Exodus 20:1–5). If you find yourself being a slave to rituals in your worship experience, it is time to set yourself free because, "The Lord has need of you." He is seeking "true worshippers" who will worship Him in spirit and truth. Notice how He is looking for "true worshippers" and not true worship. That is because it is not the event but the heart of the individual that He seeks. It makes sense that if you are a true worshipper, your worship will be acceptable in His sight.

Prohibited Worship

Within every language and people, there is a power that calls us to seek someone or something higher than ourselves. We either create objects that we worship, or we worship things created by God, such as the sun, moon, and other natural occurrences. This inner drive for worship originates from the Holy Spirit (God) who is seeking to connect us with God the Father (also a Spirit). We have given this internal member of the Godhead terminologies such as, "Something said to me," or "My mind said to me," and even, "My spirit said to me." It is the Holy Spirit who is trying to make the connection. The strength of the connection is dependent on how much I acknowledge the Spirit of God and surrender to His leading.

Do not think it strange that you are born with the Holy Spirit because God has determined that all of us should be saved: "But we are bound to give thanks to God always for you, brethren beloved by the Lord, because God from the beginning chose you for salvation through sanctification by the Spirit and belief in the truth" (2 Thessalonians 2:13). It is the activated Spirit of God within you that causes you to respond to the gospel message and to accept Jesus Christ as your personal Saviour from sin. It is the Spirit of God that causes you to distinguish between right and wrong. It would have been unfair of God to only give His Spirit to believers because it is the Holy Spirit that causes sinners to recognise that they need God and to turn away from sin; it is the Holy Spirit that prompts us to worship. God the Father has been trying to reconnect with His people since sin weakened the connection. For 120 years, He tried to connect with the people before the flood, but the cares of life and other priorities blocked the lines of communication and drowned out His voice (pun intended).

Scriptural evidence of the pre-birth installation of the Spirit of God is found in the calling of two of God's prophets, Jeremiah and John the Baptist: "Before I formed you in the womb, I knew you; Before you were born, I sanctified you; I ordained you a prophet to the nations" (Jeremiah 1:5). John the Baptist went ahead of Jesus to prepare the people for His appearance. The following message accompanied the announcement of his birth: "For he will be great in the sight of the Lord and shall drink neither wine nor strong drink. He will also be filled with the Holy Spirit, even from his mother's womb" (Luke 1:15). Worship cannot begin without the Holy Spirit, and when you decide to create your god (image), you are short-circuiting the process. Worshipping anything or anyone other than the Creator-God means you have created a counterfeit, which is a god of convenience, and the irony is that you must protect the god you created. Even though you made it with eyes, ears, nose, and mouth, none of those features can function.

The Spirit of God within you desires to worship and connect with God the Father. However, for worship to be acceptable, it must be in accordance with the principles outlined in Scripture. This is what He says: "Take careful heed to yourselves, for you saw no form when the Lord spoke to you at Horeb out of the midst of the fire, lest you act corruptly and make for yourselves a carved image in the form of any figure: the likeness of male or female, the likeness of any animal that is on the earth or the likeness of any winged bird that flies in the air, the likeness of anything that creeps on the ground or the likeness of any fish that is in the water beneath the earth. And take heed, lest you lift your eyes to heaven, and when you see the sun, the moon, and the stars, all the host of heaven, you feel driven to worship them and serve them, which the Lord your God has given to all the peoples under the whole heaven as a heritage" (Deuteronomy 4:15–19).

God describes as "wicked" anyone "who has gone and served other gods and worshipped them, either the sun or moon or any of the host of heaven, which I have not commanded" (Deuteronomy 17:2, 3). What will cause you to turn back from worshipping the Creator-God or stop short of worshipping Him? "Take heed to yourselves, lest your heart be deceived, and you turn aside and serve other gods and worship them" (Deuteronomy 11:16). "But if your heart turns away so that you do not hear, and are drawn away, and worship other gods and serve them, I announce to you today that you shall surely perish" (Deuteronomy 30:17). The prophet Jeremiah describes the heart as "Deceitful above all things, and desperately wicked; who can know it?" (Jeremiah 17:9). The heart is essential for acceptable worship, and Jesus said that we worship in vain when we just go through the motions and the heart is not in it. Sometimes we try to suppress the things that come out of the heart that reveal our true characters; but they have a way of making it to the surface. We need to guard against self-deception—thinking, "I see nothing wrong with this"—because over time, you will gradually fall away from where you started or fail to advance, choosing to remain in a comfortable place.

Be Wary of Prescribed Worship

This is where those in charge write down what you say, sing, and pray, for you to recite. Simply repeating the words of someone else is not what the Lord is looking for; you are reflecting the thoughts of someone else, but you will be accountable for your words and thoughts because one day, you will have to give an account for them. Nor is coercive worship acceptable because the heart is not in it. When a preacher tells you to "Say Amen," and you respond, why? Were the words spoken so powerfully that you had to agree? You did it out of reflex, and when the praise team tells you to "Stand to your feet" or to "Make some noise," why did you do it? Your worship should be an expression of your love for God and gratitude for what He has done for you.

In Daniel chapter 3, we find the scene where King Nebuchadnezzar made an image of gold and issued a decree that, at the sound of the music, everyone should bow down and worship the image. On the day of dedication, the administrators, governors, and local leaders came together on the plains of Dura. They read the decree, along with the warning that failure to comply would result in death (verse 6). But why did the king create this golden image? It is because he had a dream that Daniel interpreted to show how successive and inferior kingdoms would come after his kingdom (the head of gold), but pride would not allow the king to contemplate the overthrow of his kingdom, and to perpetuate his Babylonian rule, he made the image of all gold. The maintenance of power and control was at the heart of the king's actions.

God has placed a call in your heart to come aside and worship Him, and if you cannot do so in one location, switch to one that allows you the freedom to express yourself as directed by the Holy Spirit. Now, more than ever, we need to develop the habit of worshipping in our homes throughout the week and taking those expressions of gratitude to church with us (Psalm 100). For the avoidance of doubt, this is not a call to cease coming together. But if coming together does not afford you the chance to worship, you must question it and challenge the status quo. Please do not rehearse the excuse of, "I wanted to, but there was no opportunity." You alone will have to give an account for the things and the free will that God has committed to you.

The threat of punishment for non-compliance to worship on a specified day is also real and will come into force in the future. The present difficulties and struggles with sin have nothing to do with us. We are casualties in a cosmic battle between Satan and Christ, and the prize is our worship. The fact that there are so many warnings about worshipping false gods is indicative of an inert desire within us to worship a higher power. Enshrined in the Ten Commandments are warnings against worshipping false and ineffective gods: "You shall have no other gods before Me. You shall not make for yourself a carved image—any likeness of anything that is in heaven above, or that is in the earth beneath, or that is in the water under the earth; you shall not bow down to them nor serve them" (Exodus 20:3–5). We are also warned against worshipping the way other people worship their gods: "When the Lord your God cuts off from before you the nations which you go to dispossess, and you displace them and dwell in their land, take heed to yourself that you are not ensnared to follow them after they are destroyed from before you, and that you do not inquire after their gods, saying, 'How did these nations serve their gods? I also will do likewise.' You shall not worship the Lord your God in that way" (Deuteronomy 12:29–31).

Other gods

On first reading, the first three commandments appear very prohibitive, containing things you cannot or should not do. However, dig deeper, and you will see why God is so adamant. He describes other gods as the works of our hands: "I will utter My judgments against them concerning all their wickedness, because they have forsaken Me, burned incense to other gods, and worshipped the works of their own hands" (Jeremiah 1:16). Elsewhere, we read: "Your carved images I will also cut off, and your sacred pillars from your midst; you shall no more worship the work of your hands" (Micah 5:13).

Isaiah has this to say on the subject: "He cuts down cedars for himself, and takes the cypress and the oak; he secures it for himself among the trees of the forest ... Indeed, he makes a god and worships it; he makes it a carved image and falls down to it ... and worships it, prays to it, and says, 'Deliver me, for you are my god!'" (Isaiah 44:14–17).

This is a powerful image—someone praying to something that he created and looking for deliverance from an object. The work of our hands also extends to the wealth we have created and allowed to dominate our lives. Wealth is not inherently bad; it is how you use it. If you spend more time acquiring and maintaining wealth than you devote to God, you have created a god for yourself.

The Creator-God is very dismissive of those who create other gods. He says, "They have no knowledge, who carry the wood of their carved image, and pray to a god that cannot save. And there is no other God besides Me, a just God and a Saviour. There is none besides Me. Look to Me, and be saved, all you ends of the earth! For I am God, and there is no other" (Isaiah 45:20–21). The power to save rests with only one God, so we might as well save ourselves the time and effort of looking elsewhere. David backs up the Lord when he compares the Creator-God to manufactured gods: "But our God is in heaven; He does whatever He pleases. Their idols are silver and gold, the work of men's hands. They have mouths, but they do not speak; eyes they have, but they do not see; they have ears, but they do not hear; noses they have, but they do not smell; they have hands, but they do not handle; feet they have, but they do not walk; nor do they mutter through their throat. Those who make them are like them; so is everyone who trusts in them" (Psalm 115:3–8).

The prophet Elijah called out the ineffectual gods when he confronted the prophets of Baal on Mount Carmel: "So, they took the bull which was given them, and they prepared it, and called on the name of Baal from morning even till noon, saying, 'O Baal, hear us!' But there was no voice; no one answered. Then they leaped about the altar which they had made. And so it was, at noon, that Elijah mocked them and said, 'Cry aloud, for he is a god; either he is meditating, or he is busy, or he is on a journey, or perhaps he is sleeping and must be awakened.' So, they cried aloud, and cut themselves, as was their custom, with knives and lances, until the blood gushed out on them. And when midday was past, they prophesied until the time of the offering of the evening sacrifice. But there was no voice; no one answered, no one paid attention" (1 Kings 18:26–29).

Far from being oppressive and restrictive, the Ten Commandments of God are His way of saving us from disappointment and from relying on things that cannot save us, no matter how hard we try. Here is a comparison of the features of the manufactured gods versus those of the Creator-God.

Mouth

"Man shall not live by bread alone; but man, lives by every word that proceeds from the mouth of the Lord" (Deuteronomy 8:3).

"Now the Lord spoke to Paul in the night by a vision, 'Do not be afraid, but speak, and do not keep silent'" (Acts 18:9).

Eyes

"The eyes of the Lord are on the righteous" (Psalm 34:15).

"So, when the Lord saw that he turned aside to look, God called to him from the midst of the bush and said, 'Moses, Moses!' And he said, 'Here I am'" (Exodus 3:4).

Ears

"His ears are open to their prayers; but the face of the Lord is against those who do evil" (1 Peter 3:12).

"I cried to the Lord with my voice, and He heard me from His holy hill" (Psalm 3:4).

Nose

"And the Lord smelled a soothing aroma. Then the Lord said in His heart, 'I will never again curse the ground for man's sake, although the imagination of man's heart is evil from his youth; nor will I again destroy every living thing as I have done'" (Genesis 8:21).

Hands

"O Lord God, You have begun to show Your servant Your greatness and Your mighty hand, for what god is there in heaven or on earth who can do anything like Your works and Your mighty deeds?" (Deuteronomy 3:24).

Feet

"How beautiful upon the mountains are the feet of him who brings good news, who proclaims peace, who brings glad tidings of good things, who proclaims salvation, who says to Zion, 'Your God reigns!'" (Isaiah 52:7).

Save yourself the time, effort, and cost of creating gods that are ineffective and who depend on you for their creation, maintenance, and protection. The true and living God can do all that you ask and much more. And He is the only one who can save you.

Chapter 4

True Worshippers

God is looking for true worshippers, and He needs them now. In (John 4:20–24), we find key phrases that will inform our understanding of acceptable worship.

1. "Neither on this mountain nor in Jerusalem": The Samaritans and the Jews revered their places of worship. The woman was proud of the fact that her ancestors worshipped on the mountain where they stood, and the Jews regarded the temple in Jerusalem with similar reverence. However, Jesus was not concerned with maintaining the status quo; He came to set the record straight by revealing that it is not about the place where worship occurs, but more about where worship begins—in the heart.

2. "The hour is coming, and now is": This indicates the immediacy of the situation. John uses this phrase again when speaking of people hearing the voice of Jesus and accepting Him as their Saviour: "Verily, verily, I say unto you, the hour is coming, and now is, when the [spiritually] dead shall hear the voice of the Son of God: and they that hear shall live" (John 5:25). A similar time-sensitive warning is part of the first angel's message, which says, "Fear God and give glory to Him, for the hour of His judgment has come; and worship Him who made heaven and earth, the sea and springs of water" (Revelation 14:6). The hour of His judgment refers to the pre-advent

judgment, emphasising that now—today—is the time when you should pay heightened attention to the imminent return of Jesus Christ. This is the time to be certain about whom and how we worship. "Today, if you will hear His voice: 'Do not harden your hearts'" (Psalm 95:8).

3. True worshippers: It is hard to imagine God lacking anything because He created all things, gives life to all things, and owns all things, but He lacks one thing. He is looking for true worshippers who worship with their hearts and mouths, in contrast to those who simply go through the motions. "Inasmuch as these people draw near with their mouths and honour Me with their lips, but have removed their hearts far from Me, and their fear toward Me is taught by the commandment of men" (Isaiah 29:13). Jesus quoted this Scripture when He said that worship which is not from the heart is in vain.

4. God the Father is a Holy Spirit God: We have a saying that goes, "It takes one to know one," and this is relevant in the case of worship. "Even so, no one knows the things of God except the Spirit of God." According to 1 Corinthians 2:11, no one knows God better than His own Spirit, and we need the Spirit of God to worship a God who is Himself Spirit. The first act of creation was the Spirit of God moving on the face of the earth (Genesis 1:2). In worship, the Holy Spirit must be the leader because worship that does not come from Him is not acceptable to God. The apostle Paul encourages us to present our bodies as "living sacrifices, holy and acceptable to God," and to be "transformed by the renewing of our minds, to know God's will—including how to worship Him" (Romans 12:1–2).

5. "Spirit and truth": The Holy Spirit is present in everyone, whether you are a believer or not, and Spirit-filled individuals will not be deceived. To worship "in truth" means that your worship should be in accordance with the Scripture: "Sanctify them by Your truth. Your word is truth" (John 17:17). In other words, I can safely follow the principles about worship that I find in the Bible.

My Spirit and your Spirit: Do not be deceived by that phrase because there is only one Holy Spirit. "But the manifestation of the Spirit is given to each one for the profit of all … but one and the same Spirit works all these things, distributing to each one individually as He wills" (1 Corinthians 12:7–11). Sometimes, when you meet someone for the first time, it is as if you have known that person forever, and that is based on fact because the same Spirit that is in you is also in the other person. Because the Holy Spirit has no beginning or end, you feel as though you have always known that person.

This is where things get interesting. Imagine a congregation of people filled with the same Holy Spirit, as in this example: "It came to pass, when the trumpeters and singers were as one, to make one sound to be heard in praising and thanking the Lord, and when they lifted up their voice with the trumpets and cymbals and instruments of music, and praised the Lord, saying: 'For He is good, for His mercy endures forever,' that the house, the house of the Lord, was filled with a cloud, so that the priests could not continue ministering because of the cloud; for the glory of the Lord filled the house of God" (2 Chronicles 5:13–14). So, there you have it. If you want the church service to be acceptable and pleasing to God, everyone needs to be on the same page so that the Lord can show up and pronounce His approval.

In the Presence of Holiness

Being in the presence of holiness and under the influence of the Holy Spirit will bring about a change that will cause people who know you to ask questions. Take Saul, for example. After he was anointed king, he received a new heart, and after the ceremony, he met a group of prophets when: "The Spirit of God came upon him, and he prophesied among them. And it happened, when all who knew him formerly saw that he indeed prophesied among the prophets, that the people said to one another, 'What is this that has come upon the son of Kish? Is Saul also among the prophets?'" (1 Samuel 10:9–12). Here was an ordinary man doing extraordinary things under the influence of the Holy Spirit.

Further evidence of the Spirit changing the ordinary into the extraordinary is the case of the apostles when they were in one accord in one place. Their unity brought about the manifestation of the Holy Spirit in the form of tongues of fire resting upon them. "There were dwelling in Jerusalem Jews, devout men, from every nation under heaven. And when this sound occurred, the multitude came together and were confused because everyone heard them speak in his own language. Then they were all amazed and marvelled, saying to one another, 'Look, are not all these who speak Galileans? And how is it that we hear, each in our own language in which we were born?'" (Acts 2:5–8).

We do not have time to discuss it here, but the latter Scripture is important in relation to unlocking other scriptural principles. In one sense, it demonstrates the impact that people under the influence of the Holy Spirit can have on those around them, as the church grew by three thousand people on this occasion. It also clarifies something that has caused confusion over the years; it sheds light on the meaning of "speaking in tongues." Look at the clues.

'Devout men, from every nation under heaven'—People from

foreign countries. 'Everyone heard them speak in his own language'—They heard the unlearned Galileans speaking in their own language. Let us not complicate it. Speaking in tongues means the Holy Spirit spontaneously gives you the ability to speak or understand another language without having to learn it. What we often see are people speaking in unknown tongues that not even they understand. Furthermore, this is not beneficial in a congregational setting because whatever you do in the church must be for the benefit of everyone. "He who speaks in a tongue edifies himself … unless indeed he interprets, that the church may receive edification" (1 Corinthians 14:4–5).

What is the conclusion then? "I will pray with the Spirit, and I will also pray with the understanding. I will sing with the Spirit, and I will also sing with the understanding. Otherwise, if you bless with the Spirit, how will he who occupies the place of the uninformed say 'Amen' at your giving of thanks, since he does not understand what you say?" (1 Corinthians 14:15–17). If you are going to speak in a foreign language in church, you need to ensure someone is there to interpret for you. When the Holy Spirit is involved, conviction takes place, there is forgiveness of sins, He transforms lives, and God gets the glory.

Sensing His Presence

God will appear to us in a form that is not harmful to us because He said, "You cannot see My face; for no man shall see Me, and live" (Exodus 33:20). Let us look at these persons' reactions when they recognised that they were in the presence of God. Moses was in the presence of God, but God was in a form that Moses did not recognise; there was no human standing in front of him when he "looked and beheld." Instead, "the Angel of the Lord appeared to him in a flame of fire from the midst of a bush. So, he looked, and behold, the bush was burning with fire, but the bush was not consumed." This sight piqued his interest, but the Lord called to him from the bush and told him not to proceed but that he should remove his sandals because he was standing on holy ground. It was the presence of God that made the place holy (Exodus 3:1–6). Sometimes we may not see a physical form that we recognise; it may just be a voice. The Lord says, "My sheep hear My voice, and I know them, and they follow Me" (John 10:27).

Isaiah was in the presence of God in a dream, but the experience was so strong that he feared for his life. First, he witnessed worship to God and felt the shaking of the doorposts caused by the harmonious worship of the angelic beings, and after that, smoke filled the temple. All of this prompted him to declare, "Woe is me, for I am undone! Because I am a man of unclean lips, and I dwell in the midst of a people of unclean lips, for my eyes have seen the King, the Lord of hosts" (Isaiah 6:1–5). An angel reassured him when he touched his mouth with a live coal and said: "Behold, this has touched your lips; your iniquity is taken away, and your sin purged" (Isaiah 6:6). Being in the presence of holiness brings peace, assurance, and forgiveness. As things settled, he heard a call for service: "Also I heard the voice of the Lord, saying: 'Whom shall I send, and who will go for Us?' Then I said, 'Here am I! Send me'" (Isaiah 6:8).

The apostle John was in vision when he had a panoramic view of the heavenly sanctuary, and one of the first things he saw was a mighty angel who greeted him. He immediately fell at his feet and began to worship him, but the angel rebuked him, saying, "See that you do not do that! I am your fellow servant, and of your brethren who have the testimony of Jesus. Worship God!" (Revelation 19:10). The lesson in this example is that we should not worship every holy being because worship belongs to God the Creator. That said, John was still aware of his surroundings and that someone higher than himself was in front of him.

In another scene, we find Jacob, who was making his escape from Laban when he met and wrestled with a man until daybreak. This man turned out to be the "angel of the Lord," who is the Lord Himself. Jacob's life had been characterised by deception and lies, and here he was, wrestling with the God of truth. He was determined not to let go until he received a blessing. He not only got the blessing, but he also received a name change, which promoted him to be a "prince of God." Afterwards, he said, "I have seen God face to face, and my life is preserved" (Genesis 32:30). Jacob was spiritually alert to recognise that this was no ordinary man with whom he was struggling.

Your struggles might have been with the Lord, but you did not know it, and you may have entertained and looked after Jesus without being aware of it. Stay spiritually alert: "Do not forget to entertain strangers, for by so doing, some have unwittingly entertained angels" (Hebrews 13:2) and "for I was hungry, and you gave Me food; I was thirsty and you gave Me drink; I was a stranger and you took Me in; I was naked and you clothed Me; I was sick and you visited Me; I was in prison and you came to Me" (Matthew 25:35–36).

Chapter 5

The Spirit of Worship

I want to examine four examples of individual worship experiences in Scripture to see if they have anything in common or if we can use their approaches in our own worship. We established earlier that to worship "in truth" means to worship according to the principles we find in Scripture.

Abraham's Visitors

"Then the Lord appeared to him by the terebinth trees of Mamre, as he was sitting in the tent door in the heat of the day. So, he lifted his eyes and looked, and behold, three men were standing by him; and when he saw them, he ran from the tent door to meet them, and bowed himself to the ground, and said, 'My Lord, if I have now found favour in Your sight, do not pass on by Your servant. Please let a little water be brought, and wash your feet, and rest yourselves under the tree. And I will bring a morsel of bread, that you may refresh your hearts. After that you may pass by, inasmuch as you have come to your servant'" (Genesis 18:1–5).

The first observation is that Abraham "lifted his eyes and looked" and saw three men. I am calling that recognition. The first act of this worshipper was to recognise the presence of a holy being, one to whom worship is due. The second observation is that Abraham ran towards them and "bowed himself to the ground." I am calling that humility. When the Holy Spirit within us recognises Himself in the One to whom worship is due, we will humble ourselves without prompting. The third observation is that Abraham offered his guests hospitality. I am calling that service. Abraham offered what he had for the benefit of others. The sequence of Abraham's worship experience was:

1. Recognition
2. Humility
3. Service

The Wise Men and Jesus

"And when they had come into the house, they saw the young child with Mary His mother, and fell down and worshipped Him. And when they had opened their treasures, they presented gifts to Him: gold, frankincense, and myrrh" (Matthew 2:11).

The Holy Spirit guided the Wise Men as they followed the star in their search for Jesus. When they arrived at their destination:

1. They "saw the young child" (recognition)
2. "Fell down and worshipped Him" (humility)
3. "Presented gifts to Him" (thanksgiving)

In this example, the third element is different from that of Abraham, but the first two are consistent. When we enter the presence of the Lord, we will recognise Him because the Holy Spirit within us will recognise the Holy Spirit God and produce a spontaneous act of humility on our part. Today's equivalent of the gifts they presented would be our weekly offerings, as well as sharing testimonies of what God has done for us. Presenting a gift can also include offering yourself to Christ and accepting Him as your personal Saviour.

The Demon-Possessed Man

"When he saw Jesus from afar, he ran and worshipped Him. And he cried out with a loud voice and said, 'What have I to do with You, Jesus, Son of the Most-High God? I implore You by God that You do not torment me'" (Mark 5:6, 7).

This is an interesting example because this demon-possessed man lived among the dead because of his condition, and when Jesus landed on shore after commanding the waves to be still, the man came forward to greet Jesus. Keep in mind that it was the demons who were speaking through this man, and by their nature, they oppose Jesus. But you would not believe that when you hear them speak.

1. "When he [they] saw Jesus from afar" (recognition).
2. "He [they] ran and worshipped Him" (humility).
3. "I [we] implore You by God that You do not torment me" (plea for mercy).

Once again, we see that the first two elements—recognition and humility—are constant, but in this case, there were two forms of recognition—on a physical level and from a sovereignty perspective. We know that: "Even the demons believe—and tremble" (James 2:19). "And demons also came out of many, crying out and saying, 'You are the Christ, the Son of God!' And He, rebuking them, did not allow them to speak, for they knew that He was the Christ" (Luke 4:41).

In this exchange, the demons recognised the sovereignty and authority of Jesus when they proclaimed Him "Jesus, Son of the Most-High God." They knew Him from their time in heaven before He became man to redeem us from our sins. There will come a time when "At the name of Jesus every knee should bow, of those in heaven, and of those on earth, and of those under the earth, and that every tongue should confess that Jesus Christ is Lord, to the glory of God the Father" (Philippians 2:10, 11). After worshipping Jesus, the demons pleaded with Him for mercy, further adding to the elements that should form part of our worship experience. Praying for mercy and seeking forgiveness for our sins are acts of worship.

Joshua and the Commander of the Army

"And it came to pass, when Joshua was by Jericho, that he lifted his eyes and looked and beheld a Man stood opposite him with His sword drawn in His hand. And Joshua went to Him and said to Him, 'Are You for us or for our adversaries?' So, He said, 'No, but as Commander of the army of the Lord I have now come.' And Joshua fell on his face to the earth and worshipped, and said to Him, 'What does my Lord say to His servant?'" (Joshua 5:13, 14).

1. "Looked and beheld" (recognition).
2. "Fell on his face to the earth and worshipped" (humility).
3. "What does my Lord say to His servant?" (service).

In all four examples, we see consistency in the first two stages of worship:

1. Recognising the One to worship, which is possible because the Holy Spirit is present in both parties.
2. After recognition comes humility and worship.

The third stage varies according to the individual's circumstances, and these reveal elements that we can incorporate into our personal or congregational worship experiences. In the case of Joshua, he was a soldier, the commander of the Israelite army, and he is now standing in front of the Commander-in-Chief (Christ) and asks, "What does my Lord say to His servant?" In other words, Joshua is asking for his orders: "How can I serve you today?" When we are in the presence of the Lord, we will hear the call to serve, and the Spirit of service (ministry) will prompt us to volunteer.

In the preceding examples of worship, the individuals mentioned all saw a physical person, a representative of Christ, that prompted them to humble themselves and bow down to worship Him. Today, we do not have the opportunity to look upon and see Jesus or God physically. While pastors are messengers of God and we can see them, they are not beings to whom worship is due. So, how can we experience that first stage of "recognition"? All is not lost, because the first stage of worship, "recognition," can still be experienced today, even without physically seeing Jesus or God, by cultivating spiritual disciplines and perspectives that allow believers to behold Him in a personal and transformative way. Here are ways to nurture that recognition:

1. Through the Word of God

The Scriptures are a divine revelation of God's character, works, and promises.

a) Meditation on Christ's life: The Bible, especially the Gospels, presents a vivid picture of Jesus' teachings, miracles, death, and resurrection. Reflecting on these passages enables us to see and build a mental picture of Him, which we can reference through the eyes of faith.

b) Recognising God's attributes: Passages such as Psalm 19:1-2— "The heavens declare the glory of God; and the firmament shows His handiwork. Day unto day utters speech, and night unto night reveals knowledge"—or Isaiah 6:1, where Isaiah says, "I saw the Lord sitting on a throne, high and lifted up, and the train of His robe filled the temple," demonstrate God's holiness, power, and glory. By immersing ourselves in these Scriptures, we gain a clearer recognition of who God is and His worthiness of worship.

2. Through the Holy Spirit

Jesus promised that the Holy Spirit would guide us into all truth and glorify Him (John 16:13-14).

a) Illuminating Scripture: The Holy Spirit brings Scripture to life, helping us understand and "see" Christ in His fullness.

b) Prayer and worship: Through these practices, the Spirit enables believers to experience the presence of God in a way that fosters awe and recognition.

3. Through Creation

Romans 1:20 reminds us: "Since the creation of the world His invisible attributes are clearly seen, being understood by the things that are made, even His eternal power and Godhead, so that they are without excuse." Observing the beauty, complexity, and order of nature leads to recognising God as Creator and Sustainer, igniting a heart of worship.

4. Through Jesus' Work in Our Lives

a) Personal testimony: Reflecting on moments where God has intervened, provided, or revealed Himself in our lives helps us "see" Him actively at work.

b) Answered prayers and transformation: Recognising the evidence of God's grace in transforming our hearts and lives is a powerful source of recognition.

5. Through Congregational Worship

"For where two or three are gathered together in My name, I am there in the midst of them" (Matthew 18:20). Gathering with others in worship creates an environment where God's presence can be deeply felt. Testimonies and singing point to the greatness of Christ and His worthiness.

6. Through Faith

Jesus told Thomas: "Blessed are those who have not seen and yet have believed" (John 20:29). Faith allows us to recognise and behold God spiritually, even without physical sight. By developing these practices alongside a heart that remains open to His presence, we can see God more clearly and experience the first stage of worship: recognition.

Chapter 6

Personal Worship

The restrictions at the height of the COVID-19 pandemic resulted in the closure of places of worship, and when you could return, you had to socially distance and wear a mask. This brought into sharp focus the warning that Jesus gave to the Samaritan woman in (John 4:21). Jesus told her that the place of worship was not the priority when He said, "Woman, believe me, a time is coming when you will worship the Father neither on this mountain nor in Jerusalem." The time came when we could not worship the way we used to or in the places we used to, and the image of worshippers with their mouths covered also spoke volumes. It looked as though Satan, and his agencies were trying to stifle or stop our worship. The pandemic created an ideal opportunity for us to return to, or to establish, an overlooked venue for worship—the home.

For so long, we have focused on attending church to worship, rather than bringing our worship to church, as encouraged by the Psalmist in Psalm 100:4. During the COVID-19 pandemic, it was disappointing to see that most churches simply transferred their congregational liturgy online, including an online vestry. You would see attendees eating, in a state of partial undress, (totally undressed on one occasion), and others were in bed, and I am not speaking about those who were medically restricted.

On the positive side, churches were reporting higher online numbers compared to personal attendance, but no matter how you dress it, these experiences were deceptive. Supporters would defend it by saying they are worshipping, and that is because they were virtually doing the same things as when they were in church, but the difference was that they were now watching on electronic devices. I maintain that worship is not something you watch; you offer it.

When I had the opportunity to take part in services during the pandemic, it gave me the chance to put into practice the things I am suggesting for home worship. At a certain point, I encouraged the viewers to become worshippers by pausing the livestream to worship together as families in their homes, and then return for the sermon. I encouraged them to sing songs, read Scripture, pray, share testimonies, and lay up their offerings until such times as they could deposit them. This is a principle that families or individuals can adopt during the week so that on their day of worship, they bring these worship experiences to church with them.

Home Worship

I can think of at least three occasions in Scripture where salvation began in the home, starting with Adam and Eve in the Garden of Eden. They were accustomed to receiving daily visits from God, and He continued the practice after sin entered the world. I like the thought of God chasing after sinners to restore them, but they recognised their nakedness and tried to hide from Him. Recognising your sinful state is a good thing, but to run and hide is the opposite of what God wants: "Draw near to God, and He will draw near to you" (James 4:8). Furthermore, they made garments that partially covered their nakedness, which is like us trying to earn salvation by our efforts. They were still vulnerable until the Lord came and covered them fully with coats of righteousness (Genesis 3:1–21). The first couple's story presents a strong image of being in the wrong but running away from the One who has come to save you. We hear echoes of this regarding the appearance of Jesus as our Saviour: "And this is the condemnation, that the light has come into the world, and men loved darkness rather than light, because their deeds were evil. For everyone practising evil hates the light and does not come to the light, lest his deeds should be exposed" (John 3:19, 20).

Then there was Zacchaeus, who was desperate to see Jesus and had to climb above the crowd to achieve his goal. That could be you, wanting to connect with Jesus in a church or other setting, but the people there are blocking you. It may not be intentional, but their attitudes and practices are an obstacle to you being able to reach Jesus. Nevertheless, Jesus was able to see through the crowd and invite Himself to Zacchaeus's home. After their dialogue, Zacchaeus offered reparation, prompting Jesus to say, "Today salvation has come to this house, because he also is a son of Abraham" (Luke 19:9). Take courage from Zacchaeus and let nothing or no one try to stop you from getting to Jesus or to the kingdom. People who have never been to heaven will directly or indirectly try to stop you from getting there because your lifestyle does not match their expectations. Your attitude should be: "Let the words of my mouth and the meditation of my heart be acceptable 'in Thy sight,' O Lord, my strength, and my Redeemer" (Psalm 19:14). Jesus is the one to please and whose approval you should seek.

Finally, there is the offer of Jesus to come in and fellowship with anyone who responds to His knocking: "Behold, I stand at the door and knock. If anyone hears My voice and opens the door, I will come into him and dine with him, and he with Me" (Revelation 3:20). Jesus wants to be at the centre of your life. Consider this; In (Revelation 1:13, Revelation 2:1) Jesus is walking among the seven golden lampstands, which symbolises the seven churches, or periods in history. This image represents His presence and authority within the church communities, guiding, protecting, and overseeing them. By (Revelation 3:20), Jesus is standing outside the door, knocking. This indicates a shift from being in the midst of His people to being excluded from their fellowship. He is no longer within the church but is waiting to be invited back in. What went wrong? Spiritual apathy and complacency: The churches, particularly the Laodicean church, had become lukewarm in their faith and attitude. Their complacency and self-sufficiency led to a spiritual state where they were no longer fully receptive to Jesus' presence and influence.

Here is an example of what happens when the presence of the Lord is in your home, and it relates to the time when David went to collect the captured Ark of the Covenant from the Philistines. The Ark represents the physical presence of God among His people. The Philistines did what they thought was best and put the Ark on a brand-new oxcart, so they were blameless for not knowing that Israel had strict instructions on how to carry the Ark - that only the priests should carry it on their shoulders. At one point, the cart struck a rock that caused the Ark to stumble, and Uzzah reached out to stop it from falling and he died instantly. I used to feel this was unfair because here was someone trying to stop a precious item from being damaged or destroyed and losing his life for it. That was before I discovered the instructions given by God. There is a lesson here because when leaders fail to uphold the laws and standards of God, people will lose their lives. David became distressed by what happened and could not continue the journey to Jerusalem, and so the Ark rested in the home of Obed-Edom: "The ark of the Lord remained in the house of Obed-Edom the Gittite for three months, and the Lord blessed him and his entire household" (2 Samuel 6:11). You can invite the presence of the

Lord into your home by getting your pastor or elder to perform a home dedication so the Holy Spirit can reside there, and anyone who enters your home will sense a spirit of warmth, peace, love, and comfort.

Preparing the Mind for Worship

Sometimes we must pause or stop doing certain things because of poor health, time, or resources. But that does not apply to worship because in everything and under all circumstances, worship is due to God. Paul and Silas were praising God while chained in a dungeon, John was in the Spirit during his isolation, and Stephen was worshipping in the face of death. We need to shift our perspective from viewing worship as an event to embracing it as a way of life. If you have breath, you are called to worship. Even if you cannot speak, you can worship in your heart because the Lord searches the deep things, and He sees your sincerity. The words of the song "Praise the Lord," made famous by The Imperials, sum things up nicely: "When you're up against a struggle that shatters all your dreams. And your hopes have been cruelly crushed by Satan's manifested schemes. And you feel the urge within you to submit to earthly fears. Don't let the faith you are standing in seem to disappear Praise the Lord, He can work through those who praise Him. Praise the Lord, for our God inhabits praise." (Words and music by Michael Hudson and Elliott Bannister. Publishers, Songtrust Avenue.) Do not let your difficulties shut your mouth; do not let the rocks out-praise you.

Look at how these worshippers reacted to tragedy and see if you can learn anything from them. In (2 Kings 4:8–36), we find the story of Elisha and the Shunammite woman. Whenever Elisha and his assistant Gehazi were in town, they would stop by this couple's home. The Bible describes her as "notable," so they had means. Because of that, she appealed to her husband to build a bedsit so that Elisha would have privacy, and as a mark of appreciation, Elisha wondered what he could do for them, but she said, "We're good." Gehazi told Elisha that they were childless but advanced in years, so Elisha promised the woman that she would embrace a son by this time next year and, true to his word, she had a son. One day the son went out with his father but began to complain about his head, so his father sent him home where he rested in his mother's arms until he died. It is worth noting that she did not place the lifeless body in her room or his own room, but she placed him on the bed in Elisha's room. She must have reasoned that since the journey began with the Man of God, the resolution also rested with him. Her next reaction is also worthy of note.

Put yourself in the picture. Your only son, born late in life, has just died. Wouldn't you call for your husband to come home to take care of matters? Not this worshipper. She was clear about how this thing started and knew that the Man of God would also resolve it. She was confident that "He who has begun a good work in you will complete it until the day of Jesus Christ" (Philippians 1:6). All she did was to ask for a donkey and a rider to, "Go to the Man of God and come back." That is confidence and faith right there. Even when her husband queried the reason for the visit, stating it was neither a Sabbath nor new moon, all she said was, "It is well." She was convinced that her son would be alive before the end of the day. We read about her in (2 Kings 4), but she is a (Proverbs 31) woman, not bothering her husband with something she can take care of. Things get even more interesting because Elisha saw her coming in the distance and sent Gehazi to meet her with three specific questions: "How is it with you, how is it with your husband, and how is it with the child?" To which she replied, "It is well." But we know that the son is dead, yet she said, "It is well." She has full confidence in Elisha, and I also get the strong impression that even if things did not work out the way she expected, it would still be well with her. Her attitude is, "Regardless of what happens, I'm trusting God." The story concludes with Elisha restoring her son to life. Your situation may not work out the same, but when you know and trust God, you will have the peace of mind to know and say, "It is well."

She displayed the same confidence of the three Hebrew boys in the "seven-times hotter" furnace in Babylon: "O Nebuchadnezzar, we have no need to answer you in this matter. If that is the case, our God whom we serve is able to deliver us from the burning fiery furnace, and He will deliver us from your hand, O king. But if not, let it be known to you, O king, that we do not serve your gods, nor will we worship the gold image which you have set up" (Daniel 3:16–18).

Hymns for Healing

Her story reminds me of the lyrics of two hymns. The first is "It Is Well with My Soul," and it speaks about sorrows coming into your life "like sea billows," one after the other, in rapid succession. The writer Philip P. Bliss goes on to say, "Whatever my lot, Thou hast taught me to say, it is well, it is well, with my soul." The other hymn is "Be Still, My Soul" and it makes powerful reading:

"Be still, my soul: The Lord is on thy side. Bear patiently the cross of grief or pain. Leave to thy God to order and provide. In every change He faithful will remain. Be still, my soul: Thy best, thy heavenly Friend, through thorny ways leads to a joyful end. (Katharina von Schlegel, b. 1697; trans. by Jane Borthwick, 1813–1897.)

Detractors have said that hymns are old-fashioned, but put yourself in these lyrics, and feel the hope and comfort they bring. In the same way that the Holy Spirit inspired the writers of the Bible, He also inspired the great hymn writers of the past. The fact that their lyrics are as powerful today as they were in the past is evidence of that.

A troubled mind is a hindrance to worship, so whether you are on your own or in a congregation, your mind must be at ease; otherwise, you cannot connect with the Holy Spirit, and whatever you do will be in vain. A mind that is at ease is also essential for one's imagination to function, because worship is about allowing your spiritual imagination to lift your thoughts heavenwards and to give you a lofty view of God, who He is, and what He has done. The hymn "How Great Thou Art" comes to mind:

> "Oh Lord, my God when I, in awesome wonder
> Consider all the worlds Thy hands have made I see the
> stars, I hear the rolling thunder, Thy power throughout
> the universe displayed. Then sings my soul, my Saviour
> God to Thee How great Thou art, how great Thou
> art. (How Great Thou Art lyrics © Manna Music Inc,
> Stuart Hine Trust.)

Worshippers look for experiences that leave them better off than when they began to worship. It could be that things will change for the better, or it could be the satisfaction of knowing that even though things will not change soon, God is up to something on your behalf, and He will deliver you just in time. This delay is for the strengthening of faith and exercising of trust. There are worshippers who enter the place of worship with heavy hearts, and if they remain in that condition, their worship will have been in vain. Entering a place of worship should bring us to our senses and reset our minds. It brings a sense of reality and renewal of trust; it points us heavenward, and as the song (Turn Your Eyes Upon Jesus) puts it, "The things of earth will grow strangely dim, in the light of His glory and grace." In (Psalm 73), we find Asaph lamenting his situation when compared to those who do not believe, do not pray, do not honour the Lord, and yet they are "living large". They do not have a care in the world. He concludes by saying, "When I thought how to understand this, it was too painful for me—Until I went into the sanctuary of God; then I understood their end" (Psalm 73:16, 17). In the presence of God, things will make sense, and He will restore your heart and mind.

My final hymn is one of affirmation and assurance, emphasising that whatever Jesus does, He does it well and will continue to the end:

> "All the way my Saviour leads me. What have I to ask beside? Can I doubt His tender mercy, Who through life has been my guide? Heavenly peace, divinest comfort, Here by faith in Him to dwell. For I know whate'er befall me, Jesus doeth all things well. (Richard Mullins © Capitol Christian Music Group, Capitol CMG Publishing, Universal Music Publishing Group.)

Even if you do not know the tunes or cannot sing, you can read the lyrics because the words are based on Scripture and speak about current issues as well as things to come. In addition to reading your Bible, start to read the hymns, and ease your way into the presence of the Lord.

Worshipping When Tragedy Strikes

Innocent Job

You are in good health, things are going well for you on most fronts, and you can see a bright future. Giving thanks and worshipping God is not difficult in such favourable circumstances, but how can you worship when tragedy is consuming your life, and you have lost everything, through no fault of your own? That was the reality for Job, an upright and wealthy man who hated the very thought of evil. In a short space of time, he lost everything he had, except his wife and the four servants who brought him news of each calamity. Job was an innocent man, selected for the test by God, who knew what He was going to do to restore everything that Job lost and much more besides. But Job did not know that. How do you maintain the lines of communication when you are clinging to life? It helps if you are a worshipper, like Job. Before the losses, he offered intercessory sacrifices for his ten children, who each took it in turns to have a feast every day. He was interceding for his children, but who was looking out for him? On the face of it, no one, because we can only see what is happening in front of us. This is how Job reacted to the multiple tragedies: "At this, Job got up and tore his robe and shaved his head. Then he fell to the ground in worship and said: 'Naked I came from my mother's womb, and naked I will depart. The Lord gave and the Lord has taken away; may the name of the Lord be praised.' In all this, Job did not sin by charging God with wrongdoing" (Job 1:20–22).

Job's first action was to humble himself and worship because a worshipper knows the source of everything he or she has. "Every good gift and every perfect gift is from above and comes down from the Father of lights" (James 1:17). Losses are harder to take when we claim ownership, but we are only stewards, custodians, and managers of these things, and painful though the losses are, the Spirit within us will bring about a peace that is beyond our usual understanding. When your mind can come to terms with the temporary nature of all you have, including your life, you are more able to keep things in perspective.

The thinking in Job's time was that if you were suffering calamity, it was because you committed sins and you are now reaping the consequences. But go behind the scenes, and you will discover that God volunteered Job for these trials. He did this because He knew Job's attitude, that whatever happened, he would remain faithful. Satan even suggested that the reason for Job's faithfulness was because of the blessings from God. Put yourself in the story. Could it be that God is exercising confidence in you by permitting certain trials to come your way? Job passed the first test, and in round two God raised the stakes by allowing Satan to afflict Job, physically, although he could not take his life. Painful sores covered Job's body from head to toe and this was the last straw for his wife because she advised him to, "Curse God and die." I am not pronouncing judgement on Mrs Job because her words were no doubt impacted by the scale of the losses and having just buried ten children.

I am noticing the restriction that God placed on Satan: "And the Lord said to Satan, 'Behold, he is in your hand, but spare his life'" (Job 2:6). This is similar the restriction that Satan faced in the Garden of Eden because there was only one location in which he could operate. We find it in the warning given to Adam: "And the Lord God commanded the man, saying, 'Of every tree of the garden you may freely eat; but of the tree of the knowledge of good and evil you shall not eat, for in the day that you eat of it you shall surely die.'" (Genesis 2:16). God has initiated a "trial endurance cap" because, "No temptation has overtaken you except such as is common to man; but God is faithful, who will not allow you to be tempted beyond what you are able, but with the temptation will also make the way of escape, that you may be able to bear it," (1 Corinthians 10:13).

This story ends with Job having ten more children and doubling the size of his estate. Therefore, when calamity comes your way, allow the Spirit of God to usher you into God's presence, and He will help you to make sense of it all, or at least to accept it. Satan did raise a valid point that we need to consider in our situations: Am I serving God because of His blessings, and will I still do so if I lose it all? Facing tragedy and calamity as a believer can be deeply challenging, but the Bible offers guidance and encouragement to help us navigate such seasons and remain faithful to God. Here are some perspectives to consider:

> Isaiah 55:8-9 reminds us that God's thoughts and ways are higher than ours. While we may not understand why certain events occur, we can trust in His greater plan and purposes. Calamities often remind us that we live in a fallen world marred by sin (Romans 8:20-22). This brokenness is not from God but a consequence of humanity's separation from Him.

Ask yourself why you are serving God. Your reasons should stem from your love for Him, not based on blessings or favourable conditions. Don't forget to reflect on God's attributes—His love, faithfulness, and mercy. Malachi 3:6 says, "For I am the Lord, I do not change." Serving Him is a response to His unchanging goodness, even amid trials.

How do we maintain faithfulness in difficult times? We can bring our doubts to God. Psalm 34:18 assures us, "The Lord is near to those who have a broken heart." We can cling to Scriptures that affirm God's presence and care, such as (Romans 8:28), which says, "And we know that all things work together for good to those who love God." Finally, you can surround yourself with other believers who can encourage and pray with you. Galatians 6:2 encourages us to "bear one another's burdens." Finally, Paul reminds us in (2 Corinthians 4:17-18) that our trials are temporary compared to the eternal glory awaiting us.

Guilty David (2 Samuel 11)

David was the king of Israel and Judah, and at the time of this story, his army was on deployment, but he remained at home. He should have been with his men on the battlefield, but idleness made him stay behind. One evening, David got up from his bed and walked around on the roof of his palace, and from this vantage point, he saw a woman bathing. The woman was beautiful, and David made enquiries to find out who she was; they told him that she was Bathsheba, the daughter of Eliam and the wife of Uriah the Hittite. Despite knowing she was married, David sent messengers to bring Bathsheba to him. He slept with her, and she later discovered that she was pregnant.

When she informed David of her situation, he plotted a scheme to cover up his sin. He started by recalling Uriah and encouraging him to rest before spending time with his wife, hoping that everyone would believe that the child was Uriah's, but Uriah's conscience would not allow him to go home, especially when his colleagues were on the battlefield in difficult conditions. His faithfulness to his service to the king resulted in him sleeping at the door of David's house instead of going home.

David's original strategy failed spectacularly, so now he raised the stakes by getting Uriah to take his death sentence in a message to Joab, his commander. The message told Joab to place Uriah in the fiercest part of the battle and to expose him, knowing it would result in his death. David must have felt he was in the clear, but we are never out of God's sight. God dispatched the prophet Nathan to visit David with a message of reproof, but Nathan did not just come with a, "You did wrong, and now you must pay the price," message. Instead, he told David of the unjust treatment of a poor man by a rich man who took the poor man's only lamb to entertain his visitors, instead of taking one from his extensive stock. In his anger, David said that the man who did this would die, and he was determined that his estate was to pay back four times the value.

He pronounced the strongest punishment he could conceive but then four words from Nathan came as a dagger to David's heart: "You are the man." David had made the case for the prosecution and handed down the sentence on himself. But, in an act of mercy, Nathan assured him that he would not die, but he would suffer the consequences of his actions. His sin was in secret, but his punishment would be public. The child became ill, and for seven days, David shut himself away and refrained from eating, hoping the Lord would make the child well again. But he died on the seventh day. Then David arose, washed himself, and went to the house of the Lord to worship.

There will be times in your life when you are on life's floor and become disconsolate. Under these circumstances, you may feel unable or lacking motivation to worship, but that is the voice of the devil trying to keep you away from God. David multiplied his sins, but God was merciful; He forgave him and spared his life. It was this incident that inspired David to pen (Psalm 51), a public expression of his private worship, where he acknowledged his sins and pleaded for the Lord to blot them out. He requested a renewed heart and for the Spirit of God to remain with him. Worship happens when you appreciate the goodness of God and understand that God wants to be with you, even at your lowest point: "Though your sins be as scarlet, they shall be white as snow" (Isaiah 1:18).

There is an important phrase in this story, and you might miss its significance if you read it too quickly. It says, "The Lord has also put away your sins" (2 Samuel 12:13). David had earlier confessed that he had sinned against the Lord, and Nathan said because he had done that "The Lord has also put away your sins." The phrase reinforces the covenant and promise that says, "If [when] we confess our sins, He is faithful and just to forgive us our sins and to cleanse us from all unrighteousness" (1 John 1:9). Unless you are willing to admit your sins, there is nothing that the Lord can do for you. Satan's plan to make you feel unworthy and beyond saving will have succeeded because, there will be unconfessed sins against your name in the books of heaven and which will disqualify you from entering the kingdom. However, the Lord can present you, "Faultless before His presence." (Jude verse 24). In other words, there are no open sins for which Satan can level an accusation against you.

Before we leave this story, I want to touch on David's request in his confessional prayer in (Psalm 51) to have his sins blotted out and to compare it with another giant of the Scriptures, Moses, and his blotting out request, although in his case, it was his name (Exodus 32:32). Let us look a little closer to see what the requests reveal.

Here is Moses' request: "Then Moses returned to the Lord and said, 'Oh, these people have committed a great sin, and have made for themselves a god of gold! Yet now, if You will forgive their sin—but if not, I pray, blot me out of Your book which You have written.' And the Lord said to Moses, 'Whoever has sinned against Me, I will blot him out of My book'" (Exodus 32:31–33).

Here is David's request: "Have mercy upon me, O God, according to Your lovingkindness; according to the multitude of Your tender mercies, blot out my transgressions" (Psalm 51:1).

God's Book contains our names and the things we think, speak, or do—for good or evil. When we sin and confess, Jesus writes pardon next to that sin. If we remain faithful to the Lord, He will blot out those confessed sins to leave our names and our deeds of righteousness. On the other hand, if sins remain, He will blot out our names and good deeds, along with any chance of entering the kingdom of heaven. We must commend Moses for interceding with the Lord to forgive the sins of the people, the same ones who had been giving him grief, yet he was prepared to forfeit his place in heaven for them. Let that sink in for a while, pastors, elders, and those who claim to lead God's people. Are you prepared to lay down your life for theirs? Reader, you have a choice in your eternal destiny. You alone can decide if it will be your sins or your name that Jesus will blot out.

Worship Before Requests

We have come to view worship as merely a gathering of people following a structured agenda in a service. But when it comes to people relating to Christ during His earthly ministry, we find a different picture. When people came to Him for help, they would often fall before Him and worship Him before making their requests. This is a lesson in prioritising our relationship with Christ over the things we need: "Seek first, the kingdom of God and His righteousness, and all these things will be added unto you" (Matthew 6:33).

These acts of worship were spontaneous, often expressed through prostration before Christ, kissing His hands, or offering adoration to Him. It is what Jesus taught in the model prayer; you begin with, "Our Father in heaven, hallowed be Your name. Your kingdom come. Your Will be done, on earth as it is in heaven" (Matthew 6:10). Then you go on to make your request: "Give us this day our daily bread."

We do not have Christ before us today, but we can sharpen our focus by withdrawing to a quiet space, where possible, to connect with Him, or we can switch off any audible distractions. The following are examples of personal worship experiences: "When He had come down from the mountain, great multitudes followed Him. And behold, a leper came and worshipped Him, saying, "Lord, if You are willing, you can make me clean." Then Jesus put out His hand and touched him, saying, "I am willing; be cleansed." Immediately his leprosy disappeared. (Matthew 8:1–3). While He spoke these things to them, behold, a ruler came and worshipped Him, saying, my daughter has just died, but come and lay Your hand on her and she will live. (Matthew 9:18). Then she came and worshiped Him, saying, "Lord, help me!" (Matthew 15:25).

The fact these individuals turned to Jesus for counsel, for salvation, or healing is a sign that they recognised His authority and power to do what they were asking. This is worship because it involves a sense of awe and reverence towards Him. Jesus could read the sincerity of their hearts and often granted their requests on the strength of their faith alone when He says, "According to your faith," or "Your faith has made you whole."

The act of sleeping and waking is a miracle all by itself. To think that the bodily functions adjust to account for the fact that you are not active, and the amount of repair and restoration that takes place as you sleep, is awe-inspiring. For example, the heart rate drops during sleep to a level that could not sustain you if you were fully awake. Who told it to do that? That is why when you wake in the morning, your first act should be to worship the Lord for His sustaining power and for maintaining the breath of life in you. This has nothing to do with your status as a believer or not because He grants this miracle to everyone. The apostle Paul refers to this renewed way of thinking as our, "Reasonable act of worship" (Romans 12:1–2), transitioning from viewing worship as a weekly event to becoming a way of life. In this way, we will be worshipping throughout the day and accumulating testimonies we can share whenever we come together.

Worship: A Way of Life

It begins with a receptive heart that will be the temple of the Holy Spirit (God). Worship begins with the Holy Spirit prompting your recognition of the sacred space you occupy, the sanctified day of the week, and influencing a change of attitude in your words, thoughts, and actions. Worship is an act of faith, a demonstration of your obedience to God, an instinctive response to the faithfulness of God, such as an answer to prayer. We find an example of this in (Genesis 24:26, 48), when Eliezer went to find a wife for Isaac. He had prayed for certain signs as a confirmation of the chosen bride, and when the Lord confirmed the signs, "He bowed his head and worshipped." He simply glorified God for what He had done. God is always with us through His Spirit, and we need to recognise Him when He works things out for us. It is for these—and other reasons—that we should begin to shift away from confining worship to a day when we gather and begin to view worship as a way of life In the same way that we should have an attitude of prayer and "pray without ceasing," we should worship without ceasing, by having an attitude of worship.

Chapter 7

Congregational Worship

The Scriptures consistently encourage the body of believers to assemble for collective worship, and Jesus did not exclude Himself from this practice. He attended synagogues on the Sabbath, read the Scriptures, taught about God's kingdom, and performed miracles. Paul exhorts us, "Consider one another, to stir up love and good works, not forsaking the assembling of ourselves together, as is the manner of some, but exhorting one another, and so much the more as you see the Day approaching" (Hebrews 10:24-25). God desires our communal gatherings, as He told Moses, "Let them make Me a sanctuary, that I may dwell among them" (Exodus 25:8). While the wilderness sanctuary was a movable tent, we are now living sanctuaries: "Do you not know that your body is the temple of the Holy Spirit who is in you, whom you have from God, and you are not your own? For you were bought at a price; therefore, glorify God in your body and in your spirit, which are God's" (1 Corinthians 6:18-20).

Our collective worship experiences often fall short because rigid service structures hinder full expression, even when we bring our worship. One year, while driving home from a camp meeting, I struggled to stay awake at the wheel and even nodded off briefly a couple of times. After eventually fighting off the tiredness, the Holy Spirit was inspiring me with the words, "Let us talk of all His wondrous love and care", from the hymn: "When The Roll is Called up Yonder." Eager to express gratitude, I raised my hand during the following Sabbath's prayer time, but the Pastor denied me the opportunity.

This experience was a turning point in my ministry, and I vowed to prioritise testimonies whenever I was leading worship services. These moments allow me to offer encouragement and prayer, rather than formal sermons.

Harmonising a group of diverse worshippers can present challenges, particularly in ensuring that everyone experiences genuine, Spirit-led worship. My experience has shown me that there are two primary groups in the congregation: spectators and frustrated worshippers.

Spectators

Spectators attend as passive observers, expecting to be pleased. Their satisfaction hinges on personal enjoyment rather than active participation. Often driven by tradition or a desire for specific preachers, they seek a spiritual high rather than offering their own worship. Their language reveals this focus: "Who's preaching today?" rather than "What can I offer?" They may complain about service length, content, or style, prioritising personal preference over God's glory. David counters, "Let the words of my mouth and the meditation of my heart be acceptable in Your sight, O Lord, my strength and my Redeemer" (Psalm 19:14).

While we should experience growth and blessing in worship, our focus must be on edification, not entertainment (1 Corinthians 14:26). The spectator's mindset is dangerous because it usurps God's role, placing the emphasis on pleasing themselves instead. Boredom often stems from disengagement, leading to absenteeism or alternative worship methods. Psalm 16:11 declares, "In Your presence is fullness of joy; at Your right hand are pleasures forevermore." Persistent boredom may indicate:

1. Ineffective leadership
2. Distracting life concerns (Isaiah 29:13)
3. Lack of personal thanksgiving and praise (Psalm 100:4)
4. Restricted opportunities for expression

Allowing life's cares to dominate our worship dishonours God, as Jesus warned. This includes internal divisions within the congregation. While we often associate false worship with idolatry, our weekly services can reflect the same spirit when we sing praises while harbouring resentment towards fellow believers. Seek the Holy Spirit's transformation, beginning with personal, consistent worship that overflows into corporate settings. This glorifies God and prepares us for effective witness.

Frustrated Worshippers

Frustrated worshippers yearn for authentic expression, but rigid service structures often become obstacles. Many arrive prepared to worship, testify, and serve but find limited opportunities to do so. This frustration became a reality for me recently. While on the US leg of our holiday, I had a close call while driving and experienced a slow puncture that caused the car to swerve in the middle of traffic while travelling at 20 mph. I was immensely grateful and couldn't stop thinking about what might have happened if I had been driving at a higher speed. I felt a strong desire to testify about God's goodness at the earliest opportunity.

The Sabbath after the incident, I attended a church where a Communion service was being held, but there was no room for testimonies. By the time the next opportunity arose, I was in another country. I approached the senior Elder, as the Pastor was on leave, only to be told that testimonies were not part of their worship service and that I should come back on Wednesday. His response left me stunned and disheartened.

I can't help but wonder: is he aware that one day he will have to give an account for words that discouraged someone from worshipping fully? Worship is meant to be an act of shared gratitude and reverence. When testimonies are stifled, an essential aspect of worship is lost, leaving those who long to glorify God through their experiences feeling silenced and disconnected.

The language of a true worshipper reflects deep engagement and transformation: "I have a testimony to share," "I lost track of time," or "A burden has lifted." Moses' radiant face after encountering God (Exodus 34:29-35) serves as a powerful illustration of the physical manifestations of being in the divine presence.

If you are unable to express your worship openly, remember that you are a living sanctuary, filled with the Holy Spirit. Though it is not ideal, instead of remaining dissatisfied, engage in silent worship, thanksgiving, and recommitment. David's words in Psalm 139:1-7 assure us of God's intimate knowledge and presence.

Our audible worship is a powerful witness: "He has put a new song in my mouth; Praise to our God. Many will see it and fear and will trust in the Lord" (Psalm 40:3). When others witness our transformed lives, they will desire the same. Paul asks, "How then shall they call on Him in whom they have not believed? And how shall they believe in Him of whom they have not heard?" (Romans 10:14). The Holy Spirit will enable worship, even in restrictive environments. Channel frustration into a renewed passion for reaching others with the gospel. Your disappointment can become a catalyst for blessing countless lives.

Chapter 8

The Worshipper's Obligations

For worship to be effective, everyone involved must share the same spiritual focus. Worshippers are not entitled to rights like members of a club; instead, they bear the responsibility of offering worship that is pleasing to God. As the saying goes, "If you want something done right, do it yourself." This principle also applies to worship, which requires personal investment and dedication.

Unfortunately, opportunities to publicly express gratitude for God's blessings are often limited to specific occasions throughout the year, despite the constancy of His daily provisions. To enrich your worship life, begin at home with regular morning and evening devotions. Reflect on and give thanks for the blessings you've received each day. This practice will prepare your heart and equip you to contribute meaningfully when gathering with fellow believers for mutual encouragement and worship.

Sharing testimonies is a powerful act of faith and a way to combat the forces of evil. Scripture reminds us: "And they overcame him by the blood of the Lamb and by the word of their testimony, and they did not love their lives to the death" (Revelation 12:11).

Bring Your Worship with You

In addition to David's encouragement in (Psalm 100:4), further instructions about individual contributions come from the apostle Paul, who wrote: "How is it then, brethren? Whenever you come together, each of you has a psalm (a song sung with musical accompaniment), a teaching (instruction and encouragement), has a Revelation (revealing something new). Let all things be done for edification" (1 Corinthians 14:26). Imagine a church with one hundred members, where each person shares a psalm, teaching, or revelation and allocated three minutes for each. This would amount to a total of nine hundred minutes, or fifteen hours—not including a sermon, offerings, or special music. At fifteen hours, such a service would extend well into the next day. Does this seem too long to spend in worship with God?

Now, consider if your church has five hundred or even one thousand members. Would this exercise become impossible? If you believe it would, then it may prompt a moment of reflection.

If being part of a large congregation relegates you to the role of a spectator, it's worth reconsidering your position. True worship invites active participation, where each believer contributes meaningfully to the spiritual life of the community.

1. Give Thanks for the Breath of Life

"Thus says God the Lord, who created the heavens and stretched them out, who spread forth the earth and that which comes from it, who gives breath to the people on it and Spirit to those who walk on it" (Isaiah 42:5). We owe God gratitude for the very gift of our existence. Without His life-giving breath and Spirit, our lives would come to an end. This foundational truth calls us to offer daily surrender to God. Our very being is sustained by God's breath and Spirit. Without Him, we would not exist. This profound reality should stir in us a continual attitude of gratitude and a commitment to surrender our lives to Him each day.

2. Acknowledge the Invisible Things

In journeys, perils at sea, among false brothers, weariness, hunger, cold, and nakedness – besides other daily pressures – I endure hardship (2 Corinthians 11:26-28). Each day brings its own risks, whether in the safety of your home, during your travels, or while at work. Despite this, you are kept safe. Begin a journal to chronicle God's protection and provision, building your faith and equipping you to share your testimonies with others.

3. Embed Your Life in Christ

"He who dwells in the secret place of the Most-High shall abide under the shadow of the Almighty. I will say of the Lord, 'He is my refuge and my fortress; My God, in Him I will trust'" (Psalm 91:1-2). Chaos may surround you, but God's protection remains steadfast. Incorporate testimonies into your weekly worship, highlighting recent experiences of His faithfulness. While past examples hold value, focusing on God's fresh mercies each day ensures your message stays relevant and impactful.

Let the Lord Fight Your Battles

In (2 Chronicles 20), we see a powerful example of what worship can achieve. Judah's king was besieged and feeling hopeless, so he led the people in prayer, acknowledging their helplessness and placing their trust in God. The Lord raised up a prophet, declaring, "The battle is not yours, but the Lord's." The prophet told the people to stand firm and witness God's greatness. God miraculously defeated their enemies without their lifting a finger: "And when he had consulted with the people, he appointed those who should sing to the Lord, and who should praise the beauty of holiness, as they went out before the army and were saying: 'Praise the Lord, for His mercy endures forever.' Now when they began to sing and to praise, the Lord set ambushes against the people of Ammon, Moab, and Mount Seir, who had come against Judah; and they were defeated" (2 Chronicles 20:21, 22). Worship preceded warfare. God's response to their worship was to bring about victory. This reminds us that while answers may not always come immediately, we can rest in the assurance that He is working all things together for good (Romans 8:28).

Be Reconciled with Each Other

"Therefore, if you bring your gift to the altar, and there remember that your brother has something against you, leave your gift there before the altar, and go your way. First, be reconciled to your brother, and then come and offer your gift" (Matthew 5:23-24). Worship offered with hatred or anger towards a fellow believer is unacceptable to God but: "Let love be without hypocrisy. Abhor what is evil. Cling to what is good. Be kindly affectionate to one another with brotherly love, in honour giving preference to one another" (Romans 12:9-10).

Sharing Your Testimony

Allow me to share two of my testimonies, chosen because they show God's long-term planning, having things in place before you need them. In 1995, a family friend asked me to function as her estate executor because she was about to travel abroad. After about seven years, she returned to the UK, and things continued as before. Sadly, she passed away in September 2019, and I began my duties as the executor, probating the Will and preparing the house for sale. In the end, I had a six-figure sum for the main beneficiary in the United States.

While managing administrative tasks, such as arranging her funeral, our boiler malfunctioned, and the engineer condemned it. We had no means of paying for a new boiler, but I asked the engineer to prepare a quote for the supply and installation, and he quoted around £3,800, and I set it aside for the time being. Before transferring the funds to the beneficiary, I arranged a Zoom call with her and her son to discuss the settlement. Towards the end of the call, she asked about my fee. I explained that I didn't have one, but that her sister had left a provision of £1,500 for me. I also mentioned that she included the option for the beneficiaries to supplement that amount if they felt inclined to do so, and with that, she agreed to give me an additional £3,500. I was so excited that I ran to tell my wife that we now had the funds to cover the boiler, but before I could finish my sentence, I received another call, and we quickly arranged another Zoom meeting. This time, she increased the total gift to £10,000 and added £1,000 for my wife. After catching my breath, I mentioned that the rest of the funds would support the radio ministry of Life Radio UK, which I started in 2020. When she heard she would be supporting an evangelistic ministry, she shouted 'praise the Lord' because that had been on her mind for a while, and now it had come to fruition.

Twenty-four years before I needed to replace my boiler, the Lord had written the cheque. "Before they call, I will answer" (Isaiah 65:24). I did nothing to contribute to this miracle, apart from saying yes to the request to serve in the beginning, and I did not know about any financial benefits at the time.

My second testimony is more current but began in 1992 when I was the Chair of our building committee, charged with building a new church in Milton Keynes. The building consisted of a steel frame and exposed bricks, and the bricklaying gang was on the job for around nine months.

My garage at home serves as the studio for Life Radio UK, but its lack of insulation makes it costly to heat during the winter months. When COVID-19 arrived and home visits were out of the question, I decided to move the studio upstairs into the living room. At the same time, I was immersed in a protracted struggle to execute my late aunt's estate, spanning over two decades, and besides being the executor, I was also a joint beneficiary, and I had made a commitment to use my share of the proceeds to convert the garage into a studio for the radio. I applied for building control approval from the local city council, which allowed a three-year period to begin the work. No one knew it at the time, but this timeframe would fall within the COVID-19 period and would delay the start of any work. Thankfully, the lockdowns were lifted, and we still had time to start the work before the time limit expired.

As the building control approval was about to expire, I began looking for a suitable contractor, but as the quotes started to come in, they were far higher than expected. Previously, I had received quotes around £5-6,000, but material costs had spiralled, and now quotes were around £12-14,000. Late in the process, I reached out to a contractor that I used when the ground floor of our home flooded due to above-average rainfall. It happened while we were away at a wedding, and we returned to find the streets in our estate with water up to our knees, and waist, at times. The garage was not watertight, and water up to a height of five inches covered the garage floor. It also extended to the kitchen. This is a testimony by itself, but I want to quickly share two miracles from the flood.

The first miracle was that I had five or six submerged extension cords on the floor that were powering computers and other studio equipment, yet power was still going to the units with no short circuit, electrical shock, equipment damage, or power outage. Only God! Despite the deadly combination of water and electricity, everything operated as usual. The second issue was that the power supply box was in the garage, and I needed to isolate the power supply for the ground floor, and to reach it, I would have to walk through water with an electric current passing through it.

I was frightened for my life, but I trusted in God, believing He would shield me just as He had shielded the extension cords. I am here to testify to of God's goodness, but please do not try this at home. Back to the main story. We had a protracted battle with the insurance company, but eventually, everything worked out in our favour, including a first- class kitchen fitter and associated trades. The contractor that did the plastering and decorating was the one I chose, and when he responded with "job done!" for £8,500, I felt better because it was closer to what I could muster. This contractor also worked on the house in the previous testimony, so I was confident it was a viable choice, but I was wrong. When he completed the first stage, it became clear that I would end up paying more than others had quoted. Around the same time, I finally completed the work of settling my aunt's estate, but just when I thought I had crossed the finish line, the story took a sinister turn when I lost money due to a bank fraud. This was a knockout blow, considering how long it took to complete the execution of the Will and how it would impact the plans for the studio and the erection of a headstone for my aunt's grave.

I summarised the situation in my heart and said, "Lord, they have stolen your money." This was my way of saying, "Lord, this is your fight," and I can leave the solution up to Him. My promise to God was to use the funds for his purpose. I could have decided to go on a vacation or buy luxury items. The bank where the fraud began refused to refund their share and suggested I report it to Action Fraud, which I did, and during multiple conversations with Action Fraud, one agent informed me that if they could not trace the fraud and the bank declined to refund, I could seek assistance from the Banking Ombudsman. This reassured me because the treatment I received from the lead bank was appalling. The online bank refunded their losses without question, and I am pleased to report that the ombudsman found in my favour, with interest, and I was able to pay off the ungrateful contractor, who failed to account for previous work I had given him. This reminds me of the ungrateful servant in (Matthew 18) who forgot how his master had forgiven him as he exacted justice from a fellow servant.

The brickwork that he did on the front of the garage was okay, but I do not do okay, especially when it is on behalf of God. Therefore, I posted a notice on a trade website for corrective brickwork and received three responses. The last one led to another twist. When he arrived and saw the quality of the work, he said his specialty was bricklaying, and it was not the worst job he had seen, but he would investigate it as part of the project. What transpired next was a "look at God" moment, because he mentioned that he had built the church up the road, referring to the Milton Keynes Seventh-day Adventist Church, where I was the Chair of the building committee. When I asked about the names of the people he worked with, he named the four members of the workforce that the church employed full-time on the project. When I told him I was the primary client, we could not believe we had reconnected after more than 30 years. When he saw the studio, he immediately said he wanted the job and would give me a great price. He was true to his word, giving me what I am sure were "mates rates," allowing us to complete the studio for a reasonable amount. We were also able to add finishes, thanks to my wife's retirement fund. After finishing the studio, I recommended this contractor for three other jobs, which he completed, and he is now in discussions with the church about their expansion plans. Both testimonies show the long-term plans that God has in place for all of us. I have expanded them for this format, but in a church setting, they would be more concise. I want to encourage you to start writing your testimony and figure out how to craft it for public delivery.

Worshipping on My Face

This book is not intended to provide a rigid template for your personal or congregational worship. To do so would contradict the central idea I have consistently emphasised—that worship should be responsive rather than prescriptive. Worship isn't about discovering a formula to repeat week after week, as this risks ignoring the prompting of the Holy Spirit, who brings fresh guidance and experiences each time we come before God. Instead, my aim is to highlight biblical principles and practices that you can incorporate into your worship, whether individually or with your church community. That said, I would be remiss if I didn't address a consistent pattern seen throughout the biblical examples cited. This is a theme I raise not with definitive answers, but with questions for reflection, either individually or in discussion with others.

We established earlier that the first two stages of worship exhibit a clear consistency. The first stage is the Holy Spirit within us recognising Himself in the One to whom worship is due. It is the second stage, however, that I want to explore further. In every example, individuals humbled themselves, falling to the ground in worship. My question for today is this: "Has the Holy Spirit adopted a more modern approach to worship?" Why has this posture vanished from our worship patterns?

Consider this: our fellow worshippers in the Islamic faith continue to practise bowing in unison—a beautiful and reverent act. A similar posture is described in (Nehemiah 8:6): "Then Ezra blessed the Lord, the great God. And all the people answered, 'Amen, Amen!' while lifting up their hands; then they bowed low and worshipped the Lord with their faces to the ground." Other examples include Manoah (Judges 13), Isaiah the prophet (Isaiah 6), and the apostle John (Revelation 1) they not only fell on their faces in worship, but they also feared for their lives, overwhelmed by the awesomeness of the moment.

I do not see God because He is not physically visible. Instead, I see the pastor, the priest, the elders, and the praise team. But where is God, that I might bow down before Him? This assumes, of course, that bowing remains relevant in modern worship.

While this posture of reverence may have faded in contemporary practices, acts acceptable in the worship of God are eternal. Bowing in worship will return and take its rightful place in heavenly worship, as revealed in Scripture: 'The twenty-four elders fall down before Him who sits on the throne' (Revelation 4:10–11).

> "Then the seventh angel sounded: And there were loud voices in heaven, saying, 'The kingdoms of this world have become the kingdoms of our Lord and of His Christ, and He shall reign forever and ever!'
> And the twenty-four elders who sat before God on their thrones fell on their faces and worshiped God, saying:
> 'We give You thanks, O Lord God Almighty, The One who is and who was and who is to come, Because You have taken Your great power and reigned" (Revelation 11:15–17).

True Worship vs. Counterfeit Displays

Today, we occasionally witness dramatic displays in churches where individuals fall backwards, allegedly under the influence of the Spirit. However, these are often choreographed performances designed to impress and grow enterprises rather than honour God. Biblical worshippers fall forward, prostrating themselves in reverence. As the psalmist declares: "Oh come, let us worship and bow down; let us kneel before the Lord our Maker" (Psalm 95:6). Paul reinforces this in Romans 14:11: "As I live, says the Lord, every knee shall bow to Me, and every tongue shall confess to God."

True worshippers fall on their faces, humbled by God's presence, not pushed backward by men. When the Holy Spirit inspires worship, you remain fully conscious and in control of your faculties, discerning truth from deception. Worship is a binary activity: you follow God's way, or the way of the adversary, where those who practice deception in the name of healing, push or wave their clothing for you to fall over backwards.

A Call to Bow Down

This discussion is not meant to elevate one posture of worship above others, for Scripture supports various expressions:

- Praying with lifted hands (1 Timothy 2:8).
- Clapping and shouting for joy (Psalm 47:1).
- Playing instruments (Psalm 33:2).
- Bowing down and kneeling (Psalm 95:6).

Yet bowing has a uniquely profound significance, with more scriptural support than any other posture. Let us examine our hearts and allow the Holy Spirit to lead us into worship that honours God in spirit and truth. The face holds deep spiritual, symbolic, and relational significance in Scripture, often representing identity, presence, favour, and intimacy with God and others. Below are key themes and examples highlighting the importance of the face in Scripture:

1. God's Face as a Symbol of His Presence
    The "face of God" represents His presence, blessing, and favour. Seeking His face is a central act of worship and relationship.

    In the Priestly Blessing of (Numbers 6:24-26), God's face shining upon someone signifies His favour and grace, offering peace and blessing: "The Lord bless you and keep you; The Lord make His face shine upon you and be gracious to you; The Lord lift up His countenance upon you and give you peace." Here.

2. The Face as an Expression of Identity
    A person's face is often seen as a representation of their identity, revealing emotions, character, and individuality. In (Genesis 33:10): Jacob says to Esau, "For I have seen your face as though I had seen the face of God, and you were pleased with me." By extension, when you bow with your face to the ground, you are submerging your identity through the act of humility.

3. Falling on the Face as a Sign of Worship and Submission
    In Scripture, falling on one's face before God is a profound act of reverence, humility, and surrender: "So when I saw it, I fell on my face, and I heard a voice of One speaking" (Ezekiel 1:28) This posture shows awe and submission in the presence of God's glory.

    Around the throne in heaven: "All the angels stood around the throne and the elders and the four living creatures and fell on their faces before the throne and worshiped God" (Revelation 7:11)

4. Covering the Face in Fear or Reverence

Covering the face symbolises the recognition of God's holiness and human unworthiness. Exodus 3:6: "And Moses hid his face, for he was afraid to look upon God." This demonstrates reverence and awe in the presence of God's holiness. The seraphim in Isaiah's vision of God's throne "covered their faces" as a sign of reverence (Isaiah 6:2).

5. God Hiding His Face as Judgment or Discipline

When God hides His face, it signifies His displeasure, discipline, or absence of blessing: "I will surely hide My face in that day because of all the evil which they have done" (Deuteronomy 31:17-18). This represents a loss of intimacy and the consequences of sin.

Psalm 13:1: "How long, O Lord? Will You forget me forever? How long will You hide Your face from me?" This cry reflects the anguish of feeling distant from God.

6. Jesus' Face in Redemption and Revelation

The face of Jesus reveals the fullness of God and is central to His redemptive work.

2 Corinthians 4:6: "For it is the God who commanded light to shine out of darkness, who has shone in our hearts to give the light of the knowledge of the glory of God in the face of Jesus Christ." The face of Jesus reveals God's glory, bringing salvation and light to humanity.

7. The Face as the Ultimate Vision of Eternity

The ultimate hope for believers is to see God's face, signifying eternal intimacy and joy.

Matthew 5:8: "Blessed are the pure in heart, for they shall see God." Revelation 22:4: "They shall see His face, and His name shall be on their foreheads." Seeing God's face represents the culmination of redemption and the eternal fellowship with Him.

Chapter 9

The Leadership's Obligations

Let us imagine a worshipper arriving at church, ready to offer heartfelt worship to God. We'll assume that every congregant comes with the same attitude. Without structure, it would descend into chaos if individuals acted as they pleased, whenever they pleased. Such disorder would benefit no one. God is a God of beauty and order—not necessarily in a rigid "1, 2, 3" sequence, but in a harmonious and "orderly" fashion. Whatever we offer to Him must come from a humble and contrite heart. Therefore, it is the responsibility of church leadership to provide a framework, a space, and a template that allows the worship service to proceed smoothly and in a Spirit-led manner.

A Spirit-Filled Worship Facilitator

It is reasonable to expect that a worship facilitator, someone who will bring everything together, must be a worshipper. He or she must be aware of all the elements of the worship experience—singing, prayers, testimonies by children and adults, words of encouragement, and offerings. These are all important aspects of the service, but they should not become an order of worship and, therefore, a liturgical routine. How they pan out each week depends on the Holy Spirit and the experiences of the worshippers. A sermon is not worship by itself but is a component of worship, and you can spread the themes across the service, rather than one block of time.

The functions of a worship facilitator are:

1. Establish the tone and set the atmosphere for worship, leading the worshippers into the presence of the Lord. You can do this by:

    o   Collaborating with the musicians to select songs that allow worshippers to identify themselves in the lyrics. Before singing, highlight certain words or lines, and make the connection with the worshippers. In that way, they will give greater expression to the song.

    o   Putting the worshippers' minds at ease. If their minds are full of the cares of life, their worship will be in vain. They may have things weighing heavily on their minds and hearts, and they need to know that Jesus has the answer and is willing to fight on their behalf. Emphasise that worrying "only makes them sick," but when the mind is free and "transformed," we can hear God's voice and give Him the highest praise.

    o   Leading by example. What has the Lord done for you in the past week? Share your testimony first so you can be one with the worshippers.

2. Be empathetic to the conditions of the worshippers and be a student of the Scriptures so you can accumulate examples of how the Lord delivers, fights, rescues, protects, heals, and comforts others. You should use these biblical gems throughout the service.

3. While worshippers are sharing their testimonies, give your full attention to the worshipper and allow the Spirit to give you the

concluding words, the best song, or Scripture to complement what they said.

4. The Spirit will point out trends in the testimonies, and when you hear two or three saying the same things or facing the same issues, bring them together for prayer. This has healing properties and creates a bond between the worshippers.

Create a Teaching Environment

Usually, children come to the front for a story, but how is a child to learn from that? How about we adopt the biblical version that says: "Have you never read, 'Out of the mouth of babes and nursing infants You have perfected praise'?" (Matthew 21:16). What comes from the mouths of babes and infants is based on a reflex. If they are hungry, need changing, or are in pain, they cry. It is unscripted and unprompted. Instead of telling children stories, we should allow them to tell their unrehearsed and instinctive stories. As soon as they can talk, let them talk about what Jesus has done for them in the past week, and you will be amazed at their answers. The point is, whatever they say, the worship facilitator should use it to reinforce a spiritual truth they can retain. Thus, when they become adults, this training "will not depart from them" (Proverbs 22:6), and they will find it natural to share their testimonies.

The Physics of Worship

It is time for the weekly worship service. You have selected and rehearsed the songs, the sermon is ready, the worship team is together, and everything needed for the day is in place, but what about the physics of worship? What? Physics includes an understanding of the speed of light and sound, and failure to grasp this phenomenon will kill your worship before you begin. Light travels at 673 million mph (approximately) and sound travels at 767 mph (approximately), that is a staggering 800,000 times the difference. Intriguingly, despite the difference in speeds, when we are near the source, they are occurring at the same time. The best way to experience the separation is to be outside when there is lightning and thunder. You see the flash of lightning, and then you hear the thunder. But what has this phenomenon of physics to do with worship? To put it simply, I see you before I hear you, and if what I see is out of place, is jarring, or inappropriate, it will impact how I receive what you are saying or singing, and it does not matter what you say or sing after that; it will never catch up with what I am seeing.

I will be upfront and say that most times, this pertains to female leaders, but men are also falling foul of the fashion police. Sometimes leaders reveal much more than is necessary, and the same can be said when someone is fully clothed from head to toe, but the material and tightness of the clothes leaves nothing to the imagination – they may as well be naked, and when these deficiencies are addressed, they are met with a couple of typical responses.

1. Man Looks on the Outward Appearance, but God Looks on the Heart.
   o I have no argument with that, but I would posit that I can see your heart as well because what appears on the outside reflects your inner thoughts and preferences. If your desire is to please God, who is looking at your heart, you will reflect that knowledge in the way you seek to represent Him. Regarding men's attraction to the outward form and the tendency for the mind to wander, I acknowledge that a

woman's primary responsibility is to dress to honour God, not to avoid someone from straying. When a woman fulfils that priority, it will take care of everything else. God gave specific instructions about the clothes for those who were to minister in the tabernacle so that they reflect "glory and beauty" (Exodus 28:2), and that principle is still applicable for all who stand between Christ and His people.

2.   Render Your Heart and Not Your Garment

o   The first point about this response is that it is misquoting Joel 2:13 which says, "So rend your heart, and not your garments." Two completely different things. To render is to give; to rend is to tear. The people were in the habit of tearing their sackcloth clothing to show their piousness, but God is not interested in this outward show of piety and remorse; He wants it to come from the heart; that is what should be torn and replaced with a heart of flesh.

If you stand before God's people in ministry, personal choice does not play a part. Jesus Himself said that the words He speaks and the things He does are all based on His Father's instructions. When you come to minister each week, it is assumed that you have a word from the Lord, but the physics of worship could kill your message before you start, and you will not be able to catch up, and even if you manage to speak conciliatory words, the image you convey will never be lost. Let me illustrate with a story, which took place over 50 years ago. The preacher was in full flow when one of his dentures fell out, and he managed to catch it before popping it back in and continuing with his sermon. Ask me what he was speaking about, and I would not have a clue, but that 'light' moment has remained with me ever since. The reason light and sound arrive at the same time is down to the brain's synching ability. In this generation, we are familiar with keeping our work in the clouds and synchronising it to our devices. The brain is an expert in light and sound synchronization because even though light arrives first, our brain compensates for the delay and interprets the sound as happening "at the same time" as we see the action.

Leaders in the Spotlight

The Scriptures provide guidance on modesty, humility, and representing Christ through one's appearance, which is especially crucial for leaders who serve as examples to their congregations. The focus of a Christian's appearance should be on modesty and propriety, avoiding extravagant displays. The principle applies broadly to all Christians, suggesting that attire should not draw undue attention or serve as a display of wealth or status. Leaders should embody this modesty as they are often in the public eye and their appearance can influence others. Christian leaders are representatives of Christ, not only in their speech and actions but also in their appearance. This means that their dress should not overshadow their spiritual leadership and the message they convey. Their attire should reflect the qualities of a godly life, focusing more on character than on external appearance.

As role models, Christian leaders have a heightened responsibility to set an example in all aspects of life, including how they dress. (Titus 2:7-8) advises: "In all things showing yourself to be a pattern of good works; in doctrine showing integrity, reverence, incorruptibility, sound speech that cannot be condemned, that one who is an opponent may be ashamed, having nothing evil to say of you". Leaders should, therefore, aim to dress in a way that reflects their integrity and reverence, serving as an example to their congregation. This involves choosing attire that is respectful, modest, and conducive to their role as spiritual guides.

God takes a dim view of His leaders who pay scant regards to His expectations when it comes to worship, and the consequences can be devastating, as revealed in these examples.

Nadab and Abihu, the sons of Aaron, offered unauthorised fire before the Lord, which He had not commanded them, and as a result they were consumed by fire from the Lord and died. "Now Nadab and Abihu, the sons of Aaron, each took his censer and put fire in it and laid incense on it and offered unauthorised fire before the Lord, which he had not commanded them. And fire came out from before the Lord and consumed them, and they died before the Lord." (Leviticus 10:1-2).

In another example, King Saul offered a burnt offering himself instead of waiting for the prophet Samuel, violating the command that only priests should offer sacrifices. The prophet Samuel brought him the following message, "And Samuel said to Saul, "You have done foolishly. You have not kept the commandment of the Lord your God, which He commanded you. For now, the Lord would have established your kingdom over Israel forever. But now your kingdom shall not continue. The Lord has sought for Himself a man after His own heart, and the Lord has commanded him to be commander over His people, because you have not kept what the Lord commanded you."" (1 Samuel 13:13-14).

King Uzziah entered the temple of the Lord to burn incense on the altar of incense, an act that only priests should conduct. The Lord struck King Uzziah with leprosy, and he remained that way until the day of his death. "But when he was strong his heart was lifted up, to his destruction, for he transgressed against the Lord his God by entering the temple of the Lord to burn incense on the altar of incense. So Azariah the priest went in after him, and with him were eighty priests of the Lord—valiant men. And they withstood King Uzziah, and said to him, "It is not for you, Uzziah, to burn incense to the Lord, but for the priests, the sons of Aaron, who are consecrated to burn incense. Get out of the sanctuary, for you have trespassed! You shall have no honour from the Lord God." Uzziah, who had a censer in his hand ready to burn incense, became angry. While he was raging at the priests in their presence before the incense altar in the Lord's temple, leprosy broke out on his forehead. When Azariah the chief priest and all the other priests looked at him, they saw that he had leprosy on his forehead, so they hurried him out. Indeed, he himself was eager to leave because the Lord had afflicted him. King Uzziah had leprosy until the day he died. He lived in a separate house leprous and banned from the temple of the Lord. Jotham his son had charge of the palace and governed the people of the land." (2 Chronicles 26:16-21). Continual disregard for the things of God will bring consequences for those who fail to honour Him.

Whose Fault, is It?

It's a new week, and you've arrived at church filled with thanksgiving and praise, ready to express your gratitude to God. However, by the end of the service, you're leaving with those same unexpressed feelings, as the programme offered no opportunity for you to share what you brought. So, whose fault is it? Is it the pastor's, the praise team's, the worship committee's—or does the responsibility lie with you?

The worship experience should be based on shared responsibilities, and no one person or group should have the final say over what takes place, especially when it leads to exclusion. Based on my experience, I can assert that most worship spaces' physical layout works against the worshipper, because it prioritises maximising the number of attendees over creating a conducive environment for worshippers to engage

FROM SPECTATOR TO TRUE WORSHIPPER

in specific activities – yes, activities, because worshippers need to do something.

Can your church accommodate you leaving your seat to "bring your gift to the altar"? The act of taking your tithes and offerings to the front is symbolic of offering yourself as a living sacrifice. You may not have money to give, but recommitting your life is more valuable. What if the deacons stand at the front of all sections, and each row started at the left, went forward to offer their gift, and came back via the right, forming a continuous circle? Repeat this until everyone has the chance to offer themselves and their offerings.

The order of service is another aspect that works against you. Services are often so packed that there is no room in the programme (or should that be worship service) for the Spirit's prompting, never mind what you want to do. I have attended churches where I could have equally been in a TV studio – they had floor and stage managers and a countdown clock. I can understand adhering to a timely format but is that taking it a bit too far? Those who play these supporting roles each week will no doubt have done an excellent job by the end of the service, but where was their worship? Their experience was one of labour, and that is not what the Lord intended.

These formats and structures may produce efficiency but where is the spiritual impact? They also require constant changes to maintain freshness or relevance. Allowing the Spirit to operate freely in His domain allows Him to produce a service that touches everyone. Our problem is that when we find something that works well, we want to standardise it, which defeats the purpose of letting the Holy Spirit lead. Somehow, we are afraid to leave things and let the Spirit do His work; we believe we must be in charge for things to work well. Leave it alone for a change and see what the Lord can do.

The requirement to conclude service by a specific time also serves as a deterrent for worshippers. Unnecessary preambles that have no role in a worship service waste a significant amount of time. I appreciate that not all churches own their buildings and have time limits imposed on them, and in such circumstances, it is even more imperative to get to the part where the worship takes place more quickly.

The true worshipper must also cope with the fact that, in most cases, the leadership team operates under a silo mentality and rarely meets except on the day of worship. A change of mindset must take place, and everyone connected with the worship service must begin to consider the worshippers and place them at the heart of activities.

The lack of home visitation is another issue because these visits are an excellent way for pastors and elders to connect with members and acquaint themselves with their specific needs. This information can impact the prayers, messages, and songs for the service. If these members have not been attending services, the visits can function as a catalyst for them to resume attendance, especially when you hold a brief home worship service with them.

As a worshipper, you should come with a spirit of worship and conciliation; always seek ways to make a positive impact on the worship experience and let others worry about things that are wrong.

Chapter 10

Jesus the Worshipper

J esus came to live the life of a human being, whilst at the same time, serving as our Redeemer, and His life reflected that of a true worshipper. As we look to transition from worship as an event to becoming a way of life that puts us in favour with God and each other, it would be reasonable to pattern our life after His. When we take this comprehensive approach, we open the door to a new way of living. In Isaiah 58, the Lord is commenting on how the people were going through the motions when they fasted and how it produced no enlightenment. He gave Isaiah the following message: "Cry aloud, spare not; lift up your voice like a trumpet; tell My people their transgression, and the house of Jacob their sins. Yet they seek Me daily, and delight to know My ways, as a nation that did righteousness, and did not forsake the ordinance of their God. They ask of Me the ordinances of justice; they take delight in approaching God. "Why have we fasted," they say, "and You have not seen? Why have we afflicted our souls, and You take no notice?" In fact, in the day of your fast you find pleasure, and exploit all your labourers. Indeed, you fast for strife and debate, and to strike with the fist of wickedness. You will not fast as you do this day, to make your voice heard on high. Is it a fast that I have chosen, a day for a man to afflict his soul? Is it to bow down his head like a bulrush, and to spread out sackcloth and ashes? Would you call this a fast, and an acceptable day to the Lord?" (Isaiah 58:1–5).

The Lord was not mincing His words, as we would say. I can

imagine the look of contempt for their hypocrisy, and in today's language, you could add the hashtags #SMH (shaking my head) or #KMT (kiss my teeth). He is not interested in that kind of fasting (to connect with God). This is what He prefers: "Is this not the fast that I have chosen: To loosen the bonds of wickedness, to undo the heavy burdens, to let the oppressed go free, and that you break every yoke? Is it not to share your bread with the hungry, and that you bring to your house the poor who are cast out; when you see the naked, that you cover him, and not hide yourself from your own flesh? Then your light shall break forth like the morning, your healing shall spring forth speedily, and your righteousness shall go before you" (Isaiah 58:6–8).

He continues: "The glory of the Lord shall be your rear guard. Then you shall call, and the Lord will answer. You shall cry, and He will say, "Here I am." If you take away the yoke from your midst, the pointing of the finger, and speaking wickedness, if you extend your soul to the hungry and satisfy the afflicted soul, then your light shall dawn in the darkness, and your darkness shall be as the noonday. The Lord will guide you continually, and satisfy your soul in drought, and strengthen your bones: you shall be like a watered garden, and like a spring of water, whose waters do not fail. Those from among you shall build the old waste places; you shall raise up the foundations of many generations; and you shall be called the Repairer of the Breach, The Restorer of streets to dwell In. If you turn away your foot from the Sabbath, from doing your pleasure on My holy day, and call the Sabbath a delight, the holy day of the Lord honourable, and shall honour Him, not doing your own ways, nor finding your own pleasure, nor speaking your own words, then you shall delight yourself in the Lord; and I will cause you to ride on the high hills of the earth, and feed you with the heritage of Jacob your father. The mouth of the Lord has spoken" (Isaiah 58:9–14).

The Lord is clear. Instead of following a ritualistic system, ditch that and live a life inspired by the Holy Spirit. Seek to do the things that are pleasing in the sight of God, and all the things that you desire, and more, will be come your way. To fast is to deny yourself physical food, and what the Lord is saying, in this context, is to deny the use of your wealth, education, social standing, or any other measure, as a means of oppressing His people. When you can do that, we can talk, He says.

I am sure that if we looked at Christ's daily life, we could come away with clues that will enrich our personal worship experiences. He was both a worshipper and the one to whom worship is due. From a child, Jesus focused on doing the Will of His Father, and at one time His parents lost track of Him and travelled a day's journey from Jerusalem before they realised that He was not with them. When they returned, they found Him in the temple. "So, when they saw Him, they were amazed; and His mother said to Him, 'Son, why have You done this to us? Look, your father, and I have sought You anxiously.' And He said to them, 'Why did you seek Me? Did you not know that I must be about My Father's business?' But they did not understand the statement which He spoke to them" (Luke 2:48–50). You might think that the young Jesus ran off from His parents, but the opposite was true; it was the parents who left without Him. Jesus simply remained in the temple, the same place where they left Him.

After His public baptism, and the approval of His Father, Jesus sought a quiet place for further contemplation of His ministry but, after forty days, the Antichrist, Satan, came and harassed Him with various temptations, beginning with food because he knew Jesus was fasting, and would be hungry by now. He also promised Jesus all the kingdoms of the world if he would bow down and worship Him. Throughout this encounter, Jesus was able to respond with, "It is written," because this worshipper was familiar with the Word of God and used it as His defence, and eventually, Satan left Him. That is worth a second look: "Then the devil left Him, and behold, angels came and ministered to Him" (Matthew 4:11). When negative things occur in our lives, we tend to blame the devil, and that is often the case, but that only happens if you give him free rein and easy access, which he will not refuse. Consistent resistance, drawing near to God, and use of the Scriptures will result in him leaving us alone.

Jesus begins His day in solitude with His Father: "Now in the morning, having risen a long while before daylight, He went out and departed to a solitary place; and there He prayed" (Mark 1:35). He had the source of power within Him, but as our example, He had to connect to the power from His Father. You would often hear Him say that He did nothing except what the Father tells Him to do. We will make plans for the day, but a better option is to seek God's plans for us each day.

Life of Compassion

We sometimes think and say that we have a spiritual gift when it should be more that we have the gift of the Spirit, because that way He can direct us according to His Will. One moment, He is prompting us not to yield to temptation, and the next moment, He is directing our worship. During our daily activities, He fills us with compassion for those in need. It was compassion for the people that caused Him to feed the five thousand. When He tried to slip away for a moment of solitude, the people followed Him, and once again, He had compassion and began to teach them. On another occasion, Jesus was about to enter the city of Nain when He met a widow who was about to bury her only son. "He had compassion on her" and restored her son to life (Luke 7:13).

In another example of compassion, Jesus took on the role of a man from Samaria. This was unusual because the Jews and Samaritans did not get along. The Samaritan came to the rescue of someone who had suffered a brutal attack. After the people from the religious establishment ignored the injured man, the Samaritan saw him and "had compassion" on him (Luke 10:33). When we look at the phases of worship, we note that the Holy Spirit enables us to recognise the One to worship and then prompts us to humble ourselves. In the same way, the Holy Spirit enables us to recognise those in need and prompts us to alleviate their suffering. This story also teaches us the following valuable lessons:

(a) The Holy Spirit is within all of us, and He will work through anyone who is willing.

(b) Christ associated Himself with the rejected; and

(c) He expects us to continue the work He has started and will compensate us when He comes back. Having compassion for someone means you cannot continue what you are doing until you have met their needs.

Synagogue Attendance

As a worshipper, Jesus attended the synagogue on Sabbaths (Luke 4:16), and while there, He read the Scriptures and prophesied to the people. From childhood, He was familiar with this practice and would confound the rabbis with His knowledge, especially as they did not teach Him. After worship, Jesus would perform miracles inside and outside the synagogue, leaving us an example of relieving suffering and bringing hope to others on the Sabbath.

On the Cross

The spirit of obedience, compassion, and service was still evident in Christ during the last moments before His death. He pleaded for forgiveness for those who were to crucify Him. He honoured the plea of the sinner next to Him, assuring him that he would be in the kingdom. He had compassion for His mother and committed her to the care of His closest disciple, and His witness on the cross convinced the centurion to acknowledge that He was the Son of God. With the weight of the world on His shoulders (literally) and the physical pain, He felt separated from the Father, His source of strength throughout His ministry, and His cry of abandonment would have pierced the hearts of those present. He felt abandoned although all of heaven was standing by to come to His rescue. But for our sake, He had to endure it. The blessings and challenges we face are not always for us, but they are meant to serve as a witness to others about the power of God.

Chapter 11

It's Not Worship

Music is Not Worship

Music is the accompaniment of life, and we find its presence at key events in human and creative history. When the patriarch Job lost his children and business, his friends came to 'comfort him,' and for a while, God listened to their attempts to provide a plausible explanation for Job's calamity, before He called a halt to their foolish thinking and challenged them with what are basic questions, such as, "Where were you when I laid the foundations of the earth? Tell Me if you have understanding. Who determined its measurements? Surely you know! Or who stretched the line upon it? To what were its foundations fastened? Or who laid its cornerstone, when the morning stars sang together, and all the sons of God shouted for joy?" (Job 38:4-7).

At the proclamation of Jesus's birth, a section of the angelic host appeared and sang a responsive song: "Glory to God in the highest, and on earth peace, goodwill toward men!" (Luke 2:14). Then there was Elisha, who was about to consult with the Lord on behalf of King Jehoshaphat, but before he did so, he requested a musician: "But now bring me a musician." Then it happened, when the musician played, that the hand of the Lord came upon him, and he said, "Thus says the Lord: 'Make this valley full of ditches'" (2 Kings 3:15-17). When king Saul experienced bouts of depression, the Holy Spirit inspired David to play music that soothed his mind. Then there was the time when the prophet Isaiah was in vision in the presence of the Lord, and whilst there, he noticed the angels crying out to each other, "Holy, holy, holy is the Lord of hosts; the whole earth is full of His glory!" And the posts of the door were shaken by the voice of him who cried out, and the house was filled with smoke" (Isaiah 6:3-4). I once felt a small echo of this experience in an old English church while producing a close-harmony a cappella group. I was sitting next to a concrete post, when I heard and felt what seemed like distortion. The engineer confirmed that everything was fine and that I was experiencing harmonics bouncing off the post. Though not on the scale of Isaiah's experience, it illustrated the power of music.

Music is eternal and will be with us in heaven and the new earth. (Revelation 5) shows us how music played a part in the responsive worship in heaven. Music is part of worship but is not worship itself. Currently, I am observing a trend where singing dominates worship services, with one song sometimes lasting up to ten minutes, due to repetition. In those same ten minutes, we could have shared at least three testimonies. The Bible tells us that we overcome the evil one through our testimonies, not the number of songs we sing: "And they overcame him by the blood of the Lamb and by the word of their testimony" (Revelation 12:11).

Long, repetitive songs can be deceptive, giving the impression of worship through loud and energetic music, and while fervent singing is good, it is no substitute for acceptable worship, where individuals express their gratitude to God in words and action. Deception in worship is like counterfeit goods: close to the original but giving a false impression. One set of people are deceived by counterfeit goods whilst others purchase them knowing they are fake because they want to give the false impression that they are living the lifestyle of those who can afford the real thing. Jesus gave this warning in response to questions about the end of the ages, "Jesus answered and said to them: 'Take heed that no one deceives you. For many will come in My name, saying, 'I am the Christ,' and will deceive many'" (Matthew 24:4-5).

The length of a song is one thing, but the content of the song is far more important because the lyrics is one way of committing things to memory. Most, if not all, of us can recall learning the alphabet by singing to a tune. Another point to consider is when the music of the song obscures the lyrics; the song has good harmonies and melodies, so we do not examine the lyrics in isolation. We sing the song, but how often do we stop to examine whether the lyrics match Biblical teaching?

The song, "In Christ Alone," contains a line, "Till He returns, or calls me home" which implies that upon death, believers are immediately called to heaven. Biblically, however, we remain in our graves until Jesus calls us home. The writer of this song says he will stand in the strength of Christ alone until the first of two things occur. Either Christ returns in glory, or he dies, and Jesus calls him home. Changing the word "or" to "and" in the lyrics would be a better understanding, but this would infringe on the writer's copyright. If song lyrics contradict your faith, omit those verses. Home is a reference to heaven, and in this instance, the song suggests that when we die, we go home to heaven. The truth is, we stay in our graves until Jesus comes to call us home. For the record, I did make a request to the writer through his publisher and received a firm "no.", and that was the end of the matter. Your only option is to omit those verses of songs that are contrary to your faith position. Sing what is true and leave the rest. The "Booth Brothers" cover of "In Christ Alone" is the standard to follow.

The issue of erroneous lyrics goes back a long way, and the most common topic is about what happens when we die, or the state of the dead. I recall the song, "I'll Fly Away," made popular by Jim Reeves, in which he says, "Some glad morning when this life is over, I'll fly away, to a land on God's celestial shore, I'll fly away." When we die, we do not fly away straight to heaven; we remain in our graves until Jesus returns to call us to meet him in the sky.

You can also add to the repertoire: "I Never Lost My Praise" by Tramaine Hawkins which says:

"I've lost some good friends along life's way.
Some loved ones departed in heaven to stay."

Another one of her songs that I really loved was a classic from the 70's and the "Love Alive" series is: "Going up Yonder" which says:

"If you wanna know where I'm going? Where I'm going, soon. If anybody asked you where I'm going, where I'm going soon, I'm goin' up yonder I'm goin' up yonder to be with my Lord."

My point with this song is that if you are up in heaven with your Lord, there will be no one on earth asking where you are. The writer's belief in the secret rapture is evident by these lyrics. When we are 'raptured' from this earth, there will be nothing secret about it. See Thessalonians 4:16-18 for confirmation.

The words of the apostle Paul: "So we are always confident, knowing that while we are at home in the body, we are absent from the Lord. For we walk by faith, not by sight. We are confident—yes, well pleased rather—to be absent from the body and to be present with the Lord" (2 Corinthians 5:6), is justification for those that believe in the immediacy of the change of status.

Death is like sleep. Last night, when you went to bed, you did not know the exact moment you fell asleep, and while you were asleep, you did not know what was happening around you or how many hours of sleep you got until you awoke and checked the time. When we die, it happens in the blink of an eye, and when we wake, it is in the blink of an eye. We could have been dead for a day or a thousand years, but it is all in the blink of an eye. One second, you are here, and in the next conscious moment, you are awake to be with Jesus if you have been faithful to Him in life.

Secular songs can also mislead. As a teenager, I loved Billy Paul's "Me and Mrs. Jones," and it took me a long time to realise that it glorified adultery. The song's appeal overshadowed its sinful message. We must scrutinise the things that captivate us, because they will become part of us, and subliminally influence us in evil thoughts and actions, or to believe an erroneous message.

Music and worship will be with us throughout eternity, and this should serve as an example of their value to God, and what our attitude towards them should be. Society has long recognised the power of music to create an atmosphere that can evoke tension and anxiety or promote relaxation and happiness. We encounter it in films, on television, in supermarkets, and even in elevators—all designed to influence our purchasing decisions. Those who serve the church musically should exercise the same level of attention and knowledge in choosing music for worship. You should discern the atmosphere and sense the opportunity to enhance the worshipper's experience with a song from your repertoire. Here is a radical thought: How about musicians stop rehearsing a set of songs for delivery next week and switch to rehearsing based on scriptural themes? It is not about how well you deliver the songs, but rather about their impact on the worshippers' current situation.

Preaching Is Not Worship

In the same way that music is not worship, neither is preaching, but increasingly, we are seeing congregations on their feet cheering on the preacher like they are in a sporting arena, and the preacher has made a big play. Sometimes, in worship services, the preacher has become the centre of attention because congregants have elevated their worship experience to the ability of the preacher to please them, and that is not a surprise because they are spectators, coming to see what is in it for them.

Call and response are nothing new when it comes to worship, like that found in (Revelation 5). In this scene, the writer John is experiencing the service in vision. He sees that the One seated on the throne, and to whom worship is due, has a scroll in His hand that no one can open (or even look at it). As John witnessed this hopeless situation, he begins to weep, until one of the elders consoles him with the news that Jesus was about to show up. As soon as Jesus resolved the issue, the elders and the living creatures all fell and worshipped Him who sat on the throne, with a proclamation of His greatness, might, and power, and with a song. Following them, the angels joined in, accompanied by a chorus of 10,000 times 10,000, and to top it off, every living creature in heaven and earth, as well as those throughout the creative world, joined in with their declaration.

If we could approach something close to this model, it would serve us well, but, increasingly, I am observing questionable practices involving the preacher, congregants, and the organist. It is a form of call and response, where the preacher speaks, the organist responds, and the congregants stand up, shout, and clap in approval. This encourages the preacher to come back louder and stronger with another soundbite, the organist responds, and the congregants raise the level of their adoration even more, and so it goes on until, at the end, they leave saying that the Spirit showed up today, but the Holy Spirit does not work like that. You may leave feeling happy and good about what you've just experienced, but ask yourself: "Did God get what He was expecting?" Where was the recognition of being in the presence of God, where was the humility to bow down and worship in spirit and truth. We all need a personal evaluation of our worship practices, and where it differs from God's expectation, it needs to change.

Congregants who readily cheer a preacher often hesitate to share personal testimonies. Preaching is a spiritual gift and should encourage and correct, leading to repentance and Spirit-filled living. However, we are finding preachers who are seeking crowd approval, diluting their message with gimmicks. Increasingly, we are hearing when preachers are inserting themselves in the message by identifying when they think they would get an 'amen.' These actions simply reinforce the spectator mentality, and all of this is the beginning of the slippery slope of deception, brought about by mingling truth and error.

Occasionally, a preacher will ask, "Can I preach it like I feel it?" No, preach it like the Holy Spirit dictated. At other times they will ask congregants to: "Tell your neighbour" to repeat key phrases. This is pure gimmickry, and it is unnecessary. At Pentecost, the disciples spoke it once, and every man heard it with the power of the Holy Spirit. Why are preachers now asking us to tell our neighbours what they should have heard for themselves? More gimmickry. If I have received something in the Spirit, I cannot transfer it to someone else, just like I cannot transfer my oil to those who do not have it. This is a basic fact that preachers often overlook in their quest for approval.

Acceptable worship requires the Holy Spirit, not external stimulants like smoke machines, lights, and loud music. It is the responsibility of leaders to ensure that the worship does not create division or distraction. Whoever stands in front of God's people has the responsibility of ensuring that everyone benefits, but a careful observation of these excitable congregations shows that not everyone benefits from what is going on around them – so what do they do? Well, they endure it. What should be a pleasure has become something they must endure. No way is this a part of God's plan, and if leaders cannot see and rectify this deficiency, they are playing into the enemy's hands.

Worshipping with Other Believers

In the sport of Cricket there is a term that goes, "It's not cricket" which is metaphorical in British English to indicate that something is unfair, dishonest, or not in keeping with the accepted norms of behaviour. I want to borrow the principles of that phrase as I discuss what God has said about His people mingling with those of another worship persuasion. Throughout Scripture God has given admonitions to His people, Israel, about imitating or seeking after the worship practices of nations that He will drive out from before them, or who reside around them.

"Take heed to yourself, *lest you make a covenant with the inhabitants of the land where you are going, lest it be a snare in your midst.* But you shall destroy their altars, break their sacred pillars, *(take control, or take the lead) and cut down their wooden images (for you shall worship no other god, for the Lord, whose name is Jealous, is a jealous God), lest you make a covenant with the inhabitants of the land, and they play the harlot with their gods and make sacrifice to their gods, and one of them invites you and you eat of his sacrifice, and you take of his daughters for your sons, and his daughters play the harlot with their gods and make your sons play the harlot with their gods*" (Exodus 34:12-16) "Emphasis added."

"When the Lord your God brings you into the land which you go to possess and has cast out many nations before you... seven nations greater and mightier than you, and when the Lord your God delivers them over to you, you shall conquer them and utterly destroy them. *You shall make no covenant with them nor show mercy to them. Nor shall you make marriages with them. You shall not give your daughter to their son, nor take their daughter for your son. For they will turn your sons away from following Me, to serve other gods; so, the anger of the Lord will be aroused against you and destroy you suddenly.* But thus, you shall deal with them: you shall destroy their altars, and break down their sacred pillars, and cut down their wooden images, and burn their carved images with fire. For you are a holy people to the Lord your God; the Lord your God has chosen you to be a people for Himself, a special treasure above all the peoples on the face of the earth" (Deuteronomy 7:1-6) "Emphasis added."

"But of the cities of these peoples which the Lord your God gives you as an inheritance, you shall let nothing that breathes remain alive, but you shall utterly destroy them: the Hittite and the Amorite and the Canaanite and the Perizzite and the Hivite and the Jebusite, just as the Lord your God has commanded you, *lest they teach you to do according to all their abominations which they have done for their gods, and you sin against the Lord your God"* (Deuteronomy 20:16-18) "Emphasis added."

These passages show that God explicitly commanded Israel not to mingle with other nations in worship and warned against the dangers of adopting or introducing these practices into their services. God emphasised the need for Israel to remain separate and faithful to His commandments, avoiding any alliances or intermarriages, and contracts that could lead them to idolatry. They were supposed to set and maintain the standards in this area.

With these explicit texts as a background, I have questions after seeing two videos depicting events at a couple Seventh-day Adventist Camp Meetings in June 2024. I do not know if we will ever get answers unless the leaders who extended the invitations will come out and explain their thinking for contracting with a singer from another faith tradition to come and sing at their worship services. At one part of her presentation on the first occasion, she began to speak in an "unknown tongue" and then proceeded to issue a disingenuous apology, saying that she did not mean to come out sounding like a madwoman. Immediately my spirit said it was not genuine because I knew that was just a brush-off, as she tried to make light of the situation because she knew that is not part of the Seventh-day Adventist worship style. I received confirmation about her sincerity the next week when she appeared at another camp meeting, only this time, it was for a longer period, and she even claimed that the Holy Spirit had given her that language.

It is fair to say that we know the worship styles of other Christian churches and therefore if you know that a church has certain practices that does not match with yours, you would do well to leave it alone. I got the distinct impression that these incidents were a rebuke to both sets of leaders for opening the gates instead of bolting them shut. About three weeks later, I saw another clip from the first occasion, in which she said that she did not expect to find the Holy Ghost in a Seventh-day worship service – a very dismissive and derogatory statement to make at any time, and especially to their face.

To the question of why import an outside musician, it comes down to attracting people to these camp meetings which are massive undertakings. In times pasts the preachers were the headliners who would attract members, but those times and personalities are a distant memory. To the question of why not use their own singers, only the leaders can answer that, but it reflects a lack of confidence in their own singers to "Draw a crowd." What I can say with certainty is that in times past, and I believe still today, this church has produced an abundance of musicians that are of the highest quality and sought after by those in and out of the church. In (Ezekiel 16:32), the Lord compares Jerusalem to an adulterous wife who prefers strangers to her own husband, symbolising the city's moral and spiritual corruption. These Conferences acted in this fashion by preferring a stranger over their own singers, and they have exposed the members to a style of worship that is not in keeping with what God expects, and which the apostle Paul prohibits in (1 Corinthians 14).

We all should be wary of open rebellions against God. He has driven out certain specific practices from before us, so why are re-introducing them? There is a possibility that people will accept this worship style as a positive thing and will want to turn away from their traditional format and follow something new, fresh, and exciting, or so they think. "It's not worship" to mix worship styles and languages - because truth and error will always equal error. The shallower the soil in which the seed is planted, the less its roots develop, and the easier it is to pluck up.

I am wondering of any of this has anything to do with ecumenism, which is the principle or aim of promoting unity and cooperation among different Christian denominations. The term comes from the Greek word oikoumene, which means "the whole inhabited world" and originally referred to the idea of all Christians working together to achieve a common goal. It come from two Greek words:

1. Oikoumene (οἰκουμένη): Meaning "the inhabited world" or "the whole world."

2. Ekklesia (ἐκκλησία): Meaning "assembly" or "church."

When combined, "ecumenical" reflects the idea of a universal or global assembly, particularly within the context of the Christian church, aiming for unity and cooperation across different denominations.

The primary aim of ecumenism is to bring together various Christian denominations historically divided by differences in beliefs, practices, or traditions. Can you imagine giving up one of your doctrines to accommodate one from another faith, trading doctrines like sporting cards? The simplest way to look at this issue is to look at households with siblings. They do not all agree but they are united by the fact that they belong to the same parents. There are exceptions, but you get the point. The true meaning of this word will be seen when we meet in worship when Christ comes again. Until then, we should have a respect for each other and that is where it should end. There may be other social issues where collaboration can take place but not in terms of doctrines or worship.

Before these mingling incidents, a trend towards more divisive worship had begun to emerge, characterised by a growing divide between the young and the old. Is there an outdated version of the Holy Spirit, and can the Holy Spirit not reach both congregations of worshippers with one message, and style? You can extend this to worshippers of the same faith worshipping in their own language groups. The quickest way to conquer a people is to divide them. This division may have been for a good purpose, but with little consideration for the long-term ramifications, and over the course of time, they take on a life of their own. I can recall a time when afternoon services involved all age groups, even though it was the younger worshippers who led out, but later the church population diverged along age lines, with no hope of reuniting.

Finally, I want to return to the relationship between music and worship. On the night of the Last Supper, as recorded in (Matthew 26:30): "And when they had sung a hymn, they went out to the

Mount of Olives." Jesus used this occasion to prepare for the horror of Calvary. Today we will sing a hymn or song and rush off to enjoy lunch. Something must change. We need to examine the relationship between worship and music. In heaven, when they sing, it is in response to a testimony of God's goodness or a victorious action He has performed. We sing too much, and we testify too little. There is a balance somewhere. Acceptable worship is inspired by the Holy Spirit God within us, and He is seeking to connect us with God the Father who is also a Spirit, and He will help us to recognise when we are in a holy place, or in the presence of God, and to influence our humility and direct the style of worship that will be pleasing to God the Father.

Chapter 12

Keep Silent in the Church

66 "Let your women keep silent in the churches, for they are not permitted to speak" (1 Corinthians 14:34) and "I do not permit a woman to teach or have authority over a man" (1 Timothy 2:12). These were not localized prohibitions but for women everywhere. So, from the perspective of a worshipper, what is a woman to do? Is she to come to church and warm the pews? she might as well have stayed home in bed. If men have abdicated their role as leaders in God's church, and the Spirit decides to enable a woman to take on a role usually occupied by a man, should she refuse the Spirit?

If humanity fails to honour and praise God, won't the stones cry out? "I tell you that if these should keep silent, the stones would immediately cry out" (Luke 19:40). I am going to use the word "alleged" when it comes to the apparent prohibition against women speaking in church because Paul, in another situation, gives instructions on how women should appear when they are to speak. I raise this issue of keeping silent in church because the teaching about it is prejudicial. The same Scripture in (1 Corinthians 14), also identifies two other occasions when people should maintain silence in church, and in the interest of fairness, I am going to call them out.

1. Speaking in Tongues

The context of (1 Corinthians 14) is about maintaining order in church services for the benefit of all the worshippers. Paul begins with those who speak in tongues because, "There are, it may be, so many kinds of languages in the world, and none of them is without significance. Therefore, if I do not know the meaning of the language, I shall be a foreigner to him who speaks, and he who speaks will be a foreigner to me. Even so you, since you are zealous for spiritual gifts, let it be for the edification of the church that you seek to excel" (1 Corinthians 14:10-12).

I want to clear up the misapplication of speaking in tongues. The gift of tongues is from the Holy Spirit and goes together with the gift of interpretation. If interpretation is missing, it is a waste of time speaking in tongues, in the church, because it does not benefit anyone. Furthermore, what we usually hear in churches is not the gift granted by the Holy Spirit, and yet practitioners of this form of speech say that if you do not speak in such unknown tongues, it is because you do not have the gift of the Holy Spirit. That over-generalisation is problematic because: "There are diversities of gifts, but the same Spirit. There are differences of ministries, but the same Lord. And there are diversities of activities, but it is the same God who works all in all. (1 Corinthians 12:4-6). The following verses shed light on the meaning of tongues: "The Lord will bring a nation against you from afar, from the end of the earth, as swift as the eagle flies, a nation whose language you will not understand" (Deuteronomy 28:49). Language is associated with a nation. "Then the king instructed Ashpenaz, the master of his eunuchs, to bring some of the children of Israel and *some* of the king's descendants and some of the nobles, young men in whom there was no blemish, but good-looking, gifted in all wisdom, possessing knowledge and quick to understand, who had the ability to serve in the king's palace, and whom they might teach the language and literature of the Chaldeans" (Daniel 1:3-4). The brightest of the Jewish captives were to learn the language of the Chaldeans. In both cases, we are speaking of a language that is associated with a country.

In the same chapter of (1 Corinthians 14), where Paul refers to "Order in the church," he also says, "If anyone speaks in a tongue, let there be two or at the most three, each in turn, and let one interpret. But if there is no interpreter, let him keep silent in church, and let him speak to himself and to God" (1 Corinthians 14:27-28). A "tongue" refers to the ability of a non-native individual who is filled with the Holy Spirit, having the ability to speak the local language without prior knowledge. If you are from Papua New Guinea but end up in the UK in an English-speaking church and you want to praise God, the Holy Spirit can give you the ability to speak in English, but if you wanted to speak in your own language and there is no one to interpret for you, you need to respectfully keep quiet in the church.

The word "tongues" also describes the expression of "speech-like syllables that lack any readily comprehended meaning" (Colman, Andrew M., ed. (2009). "Glossolalia." A Dictionary of Psychology. Oxford University Press. (Retrieved August 5, 2011). This is prevalent in the Pentecostal and Charismatic churches, but we do not hear too many voices against it, unlike the case against women speaking in church, even though they both come within the same passage of Scripture. These unrecognizable utterances are a divine language according to practitioners, and if that is your belief, then you are making the Holy Spirit out to be a liar, because anything that He does or confers is for the edification of the whole church. If the person speaking does not understand what they are saying, how can they edify the church? Such practices, says Paul, belong in private conversations with God.

Did I hear you say that "The Spirit makes intercessions for us with groanings which cannot be uttered" (Romans 8:26)? Take a break! This is referring to prayer, and as you pray, the Spirit intervenes between you and God, and His groanings remain unspoken. Paul also mentions something else that we overlook when it comes to the gift of tongues. In a church, the attendees are primarily believers, so what good are tongues to them? He says, "Tongues, then, are a sign, not for believers but for unbelievers; prophecy, however, is not for unbelievers but for believers." Tongues come into their own when you need to witness for Christ in a foreign country or among a group of people who speak a different language from you, but you can converse with them without having previous knowledge of that language. In this era when deception will become rampant, I can foresee a time when deceivers will enter the church, working in tandem with others to speak in an unknown tongue, and their partner-in-crime would allegedly interpret for them, all for the purpose of trying to convince worshippers that this is genuine and should be accepted as part of worship.

The Holy Spirit is the originator of acceptable worship, but the anti-Christ is also seeking worshippers, and he is so desperate that he will create a counterfeit to achieve his purpose. I am not accusing anyone of consciously worshiping the devil, but if you ignore Christ and His approved methods, you end up on the other side. When it comes to worship, whatever you do must be for the edification of the whole body. If you have a habit of speaking in these unknown tongues in church, you need to stop because you are misleading both yourself and others. If you insist on doing it, do it at home, not in church or in your gospel recordings. If you are someone who insists on women not speaking in church, you need to apply the same level of disapproval to all three things that apostle Paul speaks about.

2. Women to Keep Silent in Church

The common thread that unites (1 Corinthians 11:5, 1 Corinthians 14, and 1 Timothy 2), all written by apostle Paul, is the maintenance of order in worship services and the upholding of civil traditions around the man being the head of the woman. This is not about dominating women. Christ is the head of the church (referred to as a woman), and what did He do for His church? – He died for her (you and me). It is in that context that a man should be the head of the woman; being prepared to die for her.

Scripture allegedly contradicts itself when Paul asserts twice, that women cannot speak, yet in (1 Corinthians 11:5), he provides guidance on how women should dress when speaking to the church. Taking (1 Corinthians 11:5-10) as my foundation, where Paul writes, "But every woman who prays or prophesies with her head uncovered dishonours her head... For this reason, the woman ought to have a symbol of authority on her head." The covering of the head is a veil that hangs down over the face, symbolising her status as a married woman and a sign of modesty. It also granted her a level of honour and respect in society. Compare that simple veil to what we see adorning modern women's heads and ask, where is modesty and humility? Even in trying to fulfil Scripture, women are misapplying the principles for selfish reasons, although not in all cases.

Praying and prophesying are weighty matters in the worship service. When someone prays for the church, they are interceding on its behalf before God. Prophesying is the act of public preaching (ouch) and teaching by inspired individuals, but there are those who would have you believe that women must not speak. This serves as evidence, if necessary, that certain conditions allow women to speak in the church. But what does Paul mean when he says women should not speak? Always remember that Paul's aim is to establish and uphold order in the worship services, and we should not allow anything that could defile it to cause interruptions. If a wife holds a position contrary to that of her husband on a matter, expressing it in the church would not be appropriate; instead, she should address the issue with him in private. Not only will a public disagreement bring dishonour to her husband and shame on her, but the spectacle will also detract from the aim of the service. In speaking of the beauty of submissive (honourable) wives, Peter refers to the "hidden person of the heart, with the incorruptible beauty of a gentle and quiet spirit, which is very precious in the sight of God" (1 Peter 3:4). This attitude is what Paul is admonishing.

Women in Context

The attitudes towards women in apostle Paul's time were shaped by a complex interplay of cultural, religious, and societal norms. These attitudes varied across different regions and communities, but several common themes can be identified:

Social Attitudes

1. Patriarchal Society: The ancient Mediterranean world, including Jewish and Greco-Roman societies, was patriarchal. Men typically held authority in both public and private spheres, and women's roles were often restricted to domestic and family responsibilities.

2. Legal Status: Women had limited legal rights and were often under the authority of their fathers or husbands. Their public presence and involvement in civic matters were restricted.

3. Education and Employment: Women's access to education and professional opportunities was limited compared to men. They focused on household duties, and opportunities for public or professional roles were rare.

4. Social Hierarchy: Social status for women was tied to their family and marital status. A woman's social and economic position often depended on her relationship to male family members.

Religious Attitudes

1. Jewish Context: In Judaism, women were important in the home and family life but had limited roles in public religious activities but excluded from the more formal aspects of worship and religious leadership in the synagogue.

2. Early Christianity: Early Christian communities, influenced by both Jewish and Greco-Roman traditions, saw women participating in various roles within the church. Women participated in house churches, supported the ministry financially, and were among the first witnesses to the resurrection.

3. Pauline Epistles: The Apostle Paul's writings reflect a range of attitudes towards women. Paul acknowledges women in significant roles, such as Phoebe, a deacon (Romans 16:1), Priscilla, a teacher (Acts 18:26), and Junia, noted as "outstanding among the apostles" (Romans 16:7). However, other passages reflect the cultural norms of the time regarding women's roles in worship and authority. For instance, in 1 Timothy 2:12 and 1 Corinthians 14:34-35, Paul writes about women's silence in churches and their submission to male authority.

4. Early Church Practices: In the early church, women were active in various ministries, but as the church institutionalised, these roles diminished. The development of church doctrine and practice often reflected the broader societal attitudes of the time.

3. Keep Silent When Someone Else Is Speaking

The third call for silence in the church is when someone is prophesying: "Two or three prophets should speak, and the others should weigh carefully what is said. And if a revelation comes to someone who is sitting down, the first speaker should stop" (1 Corinthians 14:29-30). Show respect to each other and give way instead of speaking over each other, it is all about keeping order in the worship. The more we keep things in context, the more we have a better understanding of Scripture. If there are prohibitions in Scripture against the things that you are doing, but you continue to practice them, that is rebellion against God, and there is no doubt who will lose that battle.

Chapter 13

The Seal of God Versus The Mark of the Beast

We could not cover the issue of worship without examining the subject of the Mark of the Beast and the Seal of God. Our understanding of these themes is rooted in our doctrinal position, but to avoid that, I decided to conduct an open and blind review by consulting experts at ChatGPT. I posed questions, and I am sharing their responses with you. My hope is that we can get independent explanations and clarity on these topics, so that you will be able to follow the trends and come to your own conclusion. In the first place, I wanted to find out how we ended up with two days of worship within the Christian faith. For this first question, I am asking a historian.

Q1: Good morning, historian. Please tell me how we ended up with two separate days of worship in the Christian faith, who made the change and what authority do they cite for this change?

ChatGPT. Good morning! The divergence in worship days within Christendom, primarily Sunday for most Christians and Saturday for some others (notably Seventh-day Adventists and a few other groups), has historical roots that trace back to early Christianity and subsequent theological and ecclesiastical developments.

Early Christianity and Jewish Roots

1. Jewish Tradition: Early Christians were originally Jewish and observed the Sabbath on Saturday, as prescribed in the Old Testament (Genesis 2:2-3, Exodus 20:8-11).

2. Resurrection of Jesus: The resurrection of Jesus on a Sunday (the first day of the week) played a significant role in early Christian worship practices. This event was pivotal and celebrated weekly by early Christians.

Shift from Saturday to Sunday

3. Apostolic Influence: Over time, the practice of gathering on Sunday, known as the "Lord's Day," became more common among Christians. This day was chosen to honour Jesus' resurrection. By the end of the first century, this practice was widely recognised.

4. Second Century Developments: Early Christian writings, such as the *Didache* and the letters of Ignatius of Antioch, indicate that Sunday worship was established as distinct from the Jewish Sabbath.

5. Constantine's Influence: The Roman Emperor Constantine the Great, after converting to Christianity, played a significant role in formalising Sunday worship. In 321 A.D., Constantine enacted civil legislation declaring Sunday a day of rest: "On the venerable day of the Sun let the magistrates and people residing in cities rest, and let all workshops be closed." (Codex Justinianus 3.12.3)

6. Council of Laodicea (circa 363-364 AD): This council further reinforced Sunday observance by decreeing that Christians

should honour Sunday and refrain from resting on the Sabbath (Canon 29).

Theological Claims for the Change

7. Resurrection Celebration: The primary theological justification for Sunday worship is the celebration of Jesus' resurrection, which signifies the new creation and the new covenant.
8. Apostolic Tradition: Proponents argue that Sunday worship is rooted in apostolic tradition and the practice of the early church, rather than a later invention.

Continued Sabbath Observance

9. Seventh-day Adventists and Similar Groups: In the 19th century, some Christian groups, notably the Seventh-day Adventists, emerged emphasising a return to Saturday Sabbath observance. They argue that the Sabbath commandment is perpetual and was never abrogated by Jesus or the apostles.

Summary

- Sunday Worship: Adopted early due to the significance of the resurrection and solidified by Roman and ecclesiastical authority.
- Saturday Sabbath: Retained by some groups based on their interpretation of biblical commandments and a desire to adhere to the original Sabbath observance.

Thus, the divergence in worship days within Christendom is a result of theological, historical, and ecclesiastical developments from the early days of

Christianity through the influence of Roman law and the practices of early church leaders. "Emphasis added."

Commentary: There is little doubt that Sunday is the first day of the week, but God has instructed us to worship Him on the seventh day, Saturday. Some have said we can worship God on any day, and that is true, but God only sanctified and set apart the seventh day, Saturday. The resurrection is crucial to our salvation, but God did not ask us to commemorate that day, important as it is.

For the avoidance of doubt, the Sabbath has not been changed from Saturday to Sunday because God has not made that change. He predicted that attempts would be made but only He can ratify changes to His laws, and on the point, He says: "For I am the Lord, I do not change" (Malachi 3:6), "Forever, O Lord, Your word is settled in heaven" (Psalm 119:89). Jesus emphasised that the moral principles of God's law would remain unchanged: ""Do not think that I came to destroy the Law or the Prophets. I did not come to destroy but to fulfil. For assuredly, I say to you, till heaven and earth pass away, one jot or one tittle will by no means pass from the law till all is fulfilled" (Matthew 5:17-18).

Finally, the perfection of God's law shows it needs no alteration: "The law of the Lord is perfect, converting the soul; the testimony of the Lord is sure, making wise the simple" (Psalm 19:7).

External references

1. The Didache and writings of Ignatius of Antioch for early Christian practices.
2. Justin Martyr's "First Apology" for early theological reasoning.
3. Eusebius's "Ecclesiastical History" for historical accounts of Constantine's influence.

4. Catholic Encyclopaedia entries on the Council of Laodicea and Sunday worship.

5. The Seventh-day Adventist Bible Commentary for the perspective on Sabbath observance.

Q2: Who led the drive to ratify Sunday as the day of worship, after the Council of Laodicea?

ChatGPT

After the Council of Laodicea, the drive to ratify Sunday as the primary day of worship was led by various church leaders, theologians, and ecclesiastical authorities. While no single individual can be credited with this movement, several key figures and groups played significant roles:

1. Church Fathers

Athanasius of Alexandria (c. 296–373 AD): Though he predates the Council of Laodicea, Athanasius was a staunch defender of Nicene Christianity and advocated for Sunday worship as part of Christian orthodoxy.

Augustine of Hippo (354–430 AD): Augustine's extensive theological writings reinforced the importance of Sunday worship. He emphasized the resurrection of Christ and its commemoration on Sunday as central to Christian practice.

2. Papal Authority

Popes and Bishops: The bishops of Rome, who later became known as popes, played a crucial role in promoting and enforcing Sunday worship. Their influence extended across the Western Church, and their decrees and letters often emphasized the observance of Sunday. "Emphasis added."

3. Synods and Councils

Various synods and regional church councils held after Laodicea continued to endorse and enforce Sunday observance.

4. Christian Emperors

Constantine the Great (reigned 306–337 AD): Although Constantine's edict came before the Council of Laodicea, his declaration of Sunday as a day of rest set a significant precedent that was built upon by later church leaders.

Theodosius I (reigned 379–395 AD): Theodosius made Christianity the state religion of the Roman Empire and enforced Christian practices, including Sunday observance, through imperial laws.

Conclusion

The ratification of Sunday as the primary day of worship was a collective effort driven by church leaders, theologians, ecclesiastical councils, monastic movements, and Christian emperors. *Their combined influence, through theological teachings, church decrees, and legal enforcement, ensured that Sunday worship became a foundational aspect of Christian practice throughout the centuries following the Council of Laodicea.* Emphasis added.

External references

Eusebius of Caesarea

Primary Source: Ecclesiastical History

Relevance: Provides historical context and details on Constantine's influence on Sunday worship.

St. Augustine

Primary Source: The City of God and various sermons.

Relevance: Offers theological justifications for Sunday observance.

Catholic Encyclopaedia

Entries on the Council of Laodicea, Pope Sylvester I, and Pope Innocent I.

Online Access: Catholic Encyclopaedia

The Canons of the Council of Laodicea

Primary Source: Canons addressing Sabbath and Sunday observance.

Relevance: Canon 29 specifically speaks to the observance of Sunday.

The Writings of St. Jerome

Primary Source: Jerome's letters and biblical commentaries.

Relevance: Influential in shaping Western Christianity and supporting Sunday worship.

Theodosius' Edicts

Primary Source: Historical records of Theodosius I's decrees.

Relevance: Enforced Christian practices, including Sunday worship, throughout the Roman Empire.

Q3: Has there been any warnings in Scripture about attempts to change times and laws?

ChatGPT

Yes, the Bible contains warnings about attempts to change times and laws, particularly in prophetic books. The most notable passage is found in the book of Daniel:

Daniel 7:25

Verse: "He shall speak words against the Most-high and shall wear out the saints of the Most-high and shall think to change the times and the law; and they shall be given into his hand for a time, times, and half a time."

Context: This verse is part of a vision given to Daniel about four beasts representing four kingdoms. The fourth beast is particularly fearsome and has ten horns, symbolising ten kings. Another horn, often interpreted as an antichrist figure or a powerful ruler, emerges and speaks arrogantly against God, oppresses the saints, and seeks to change sacred times and laws.

Interpretation

Arrogance and Opposition to God:

The figure mentioned in Daniel 7:25 is characterised by blasphemy against God ("speak words against the Most-high") and intense persecution of God's people ("wear out the saints of the Most-high").

Changing Times and Laws:

This attempt to "change the times and the law" is often interpreted as an effort to alter divinely established ordinances and sacred times, potentially including the Sabbath and other religious observances. It represents a direct challenge to God's authority and established order.

Prophetic Fulfilment:

Different interpretations exist about the fulfilment of this prophecy. Some see it as a reference to historical figures or events (such as Antiochus IV Epiphanes or the Roman Empire), while others view it as an end-time prophecy concerning the Antichrist.

New Testament Warnings. The New Testament also contains warnings about false teachings and changes to God's established order:

2 Thessalonians 2:3-4:

"Let no one deceive you in any way. For that day will not come, unless the rebellion comes first, and the man of lawlessness is revealed, the son of destruction, who opposes and exalts himself against every so-called god or object of worship, so that he takes his seat in the temple of God, proclaiming himself to be God." This passage speaks of a "man of lawlessness" who will oppose God and exalt himself, often linked to the antichrist figure in

Christian eschatology.

Revelation 13:5-7: "And the beast was given a mouth uttering haughty and blasphemous words, and it was allowed to exercise authority for forty-two months. It opened its mouth to utter blasphemies against God, blaspheming his name and his dwelling, that is, those who dwell in heaven. Also, it was allowed to make war on the saints and to conquer them. And authority was given it over every tribe and people and language and nation."

This passage describes a beast that speaks blasphemies against God and persecutes the saints, aligning with the themes found in Daniel.

Conclusion

Scripture warns of attempts to change divinely established times and laws, particularly in prophetic contexts. Daniel 7:25 is a key verse highlighting such attempts by a powerful figure who opposes God and persecutes His people. These warnings are echoed in the New Testament, emphasising vigilance against false teachings and those who seek to undermine God's authority.

Sources for Interpretation and Commentary

1. The Holy Bible (Daniel 7:25):

   Primary Source: Any standard Bible translation, such as the NIV, KJV, or ESV.

   Relevance: Direct scriptural warning about changing times and laws.

Commentaries on the Book of Daniel:

2. John Calvin's Commentary on Daniel: Offers a Protestant Reformation perspective on the passage.

3. Matthew Henry's Commentary on the Whole Bible: Provides a comprehensive analysis of the prophetic significance of Daniel 7:25.

4. The Expositor's Bible Commentary: A widely respected evangelical commentary that provides historical and theological insights into the text.

5. The Early Church Fathers:

   (a) St. Jerome's Commentary on Daniel: Offers an early Christian interpretation of the passage.

   (b) Hippolytus of Rome's Treatise on Christ and Antichrist: Discusses the antichrist and related prophecies, including interpretations of Daniel's visions.

6. Catholic Encyclopaedia:

   Entry on the Book of Daniel: Provides an overview of the historical and theological context of Daniel's prophecies.

Q4. Who are Seventh-day Adventists, and can you summarise their stance of the Sabbath?

ChatGPT

Seventh-day Adventists (SDAs) are a Protestant Christian denomination known for their observance of Saturday, the seventh day of the week, as the Sabbath. The denomination emerged in the mid-19th century in the United States during the Second Great Awakening, a period of religious revival. Here are some key points about their origins and beliefs:

Origins: The Seventh-day Adventist Church was formally established in 1863, although its roots trace back to the Millerite movement, led by William Miller, who predicted the imminent return of Jesus Christ in the 1840s. After the Great Disappointment (the predicted return did not happen in 1844), some Millerites continued to study the Bible intensely, leading to the development of distinct beliefs and the formation of the SDA Church.

Key Founders: Among the key figures in the early Adventist movement were James White, Ellen G. White, and Joseph Bates. Ellen G. White became a central figure due to her prolific writings and claimed prophetic visions.

Global Presence: Today, the Seventh-day Adventist Church is a global organization with millions of members worldwide, known for its emphasis on health, education, and missionary work.

Seventh-day Adventists' Stance on the Sabbath

The Seventh-day Adventist Church places a strong emphasis on the observance of the Sabbath, which they believe is a crucial and perpetual commandment. Here is a summary of their stance:

Biblical Basis:

Creation Ordinance: SDAs believe that the Sabbath was established at creation (Genesis 2:2-

3) when God rested on the seventh day and sanctified it.

Fourth Commandment: They uphold the Fourth Commandment, which commands the observance of the Sabbath day as holy (Exodus 20:8-11).

Sabbath Observance:

Time Frame: The Sabbath begins at sunset on Friday and ends at sunset on Saturday. This practice is based on the biblical reckoning of a day (Genesis 1:5).

Theological Significance:

Sign of Loyalty: Observing the Sabbath is seen as a sign of loyalty to God and an act of obedience to His commandments.

Remembrance and Rest: The Sabbath is a time to remember God's creation, reflect on His blessings, and experience physical and spiritual rest.

End-Time Importance: SDAs believe that the Sabbath will play a crucial role in the end times, serving as a test of faithfulness to God's law.

Contrary to Sunday Observance:

Historical View: *SDAs hold that the change from Saturday to Sunday worship, made by early Christian leaders and later formalized by Roman Emperor Constantine and church councils, lacks biblical authority.* "Emphasis added."

Sources for Further Study

1. The Holy Bible:

    Primary Source: For biblical commandments and practices regarding the Sabbath.

    Relevance: Provides the scriptural basis for Sabbath observance.

2. Ellen G. White's Writings:

    (a) "The Great Controversy": Discusses the history and significance of the Sabbath.

    (b) "Steps to Christ": Offers insights into Adventist theology and practice.

3. Seventh-day Adventist Church Publications

   (a) "Seventh-day Adventists Believe": A comprehensive overview of the church's doctrines.

   (b) "The Sabbath in Scripture and History": Explores the biblical and historical aspects of Sabbath observance.

4. Historical Context:

   (a) "From Sabbath to Sunday" by Samuele Bacchiocchi: Examines the historical transition of Sabbath observance to Sunday.

   (b) Catholic Encyclopaedia: Provides historical context on changes in Christian practices. Catholic Encyclopaedia on Sunday

Q5: For the avoidance of doubt, please list the top ten worldwide denominations (starting with the largest) in a table and organise as follows.

Column 1 = name of denomination
Column 2 = membership
Column 3 = annual income

ChatGPT

Certainly! Below is a table listing the top ten worldwide Christian denominations, starting with the largest. The membership figures are based on the most recent available data, while annual income figures are estimates, as exact financial data can vary and may not be publicly disclosed for all denominations.

Name of Denomination	Membership	Estimated Annual Income (USD)
Roman Catholic Church	1.3 billion	$5 billion
Anglican Communion	85 million	$1.1 billion
Lutheran World Federation	75 million	$1 billion
Assemblies of God	69 million	$2 billion
Seventh-day Adventist Church	21 million	$3.5 billion
Church of Jesus Christ of Latter-day Saints (Mormon)	16.6 million	$7 billion
Southern Baptist Convention	14.8 million	$11 billion
United Methodist Church	12.7 million	$6.3 billion
Pentecostal World Fellowship	10 million	$1 billion
Presbyterian Church (USA)	1.2 million	$2 billion

Considerations:

Membership Figures: These are approximate and can fluctuate based on the latest surveys and self-reported data by the denominations.

Annual Income: Exact financial figures can be difficult to determine due to the decentralized nature of some denominations and differences in financial reporting practices. The estimates provided are based on available data and reputable sources.

These figures present the denominations in descending order of membership while also providing an estimate of their financial scope.

Source: Wikipedia List of Christian denominations by number of members.

Follow-up question: Some people have labelled the Seventh-day Adventist Church as a cult, is that a fair characterisation?

ChatGPT

The Seventh-day Adventist Church is not considered a cult by mainstream religious scholars and sociologists. It is a legitimate Christian denomination with a worldwide membership of millions. Here is a breakdown of why it is not labelled as a cult:

1. Orthodox Christian Beliefs: The Seventh-day Adventist Church holds many essential Christian beliefs, such as the Trinity, the divinity of Jesus Christ, and salvation by grace through faith.

2. Established Structure: The church has a well-organised and transparent structure with established doctrines, a clear leadership hierarchy, and regular democratic processes for decision-making.

3. Freedom of Worship: Members of the Seventh-day Adventist Church are free to leave the denomination without fear of retribution or ostracism, which is a key characteristic that differentiates it from cults.

4. Public Engagement: The church operates openly and is involved in various public activities, including health care, education, and humanitarian aid, reflecting its commitment to social welfare and community service.

5. Academic Recognition: The church's institutions, such as hospitals and universities, are accredited and respected in their respective fields.

However, the term "cult" can be subjective and is sometimes used pejoratively (with contempt or disapproval) to describe any group with beliefs or practices that differ significantly from mainstream or traditional views. Some critics may use the term to describe the Seventh-day Adventist Church due to its distinctive beliefs, such as the observance of Saturday as the Sabbath, emphasis on the imminent Second Coming of Christ, and dietary guidelines. It is important to consider the specific criteria and context when evaluating whether a religious group is a cult. The Seventh-day Adventist Church, while having unique doctrines and practices, does not meet the criteria of a cult in the academic or sociological sense.

Cult Characteristics

1. Authoritarian Leadership

    Centralised Authority: A single leader or small group exercises complete control.

    Charismatic Leadership: The leader is often seen as infallible, possessing special knowledge, or divinely inspired.

    Unquestioning Obedience: Members are expected to obey the leader without question.

2. Exclusive Beliefs

    Claim to Special Truth: The group asserts it has exclusive access to ultimate truth or salvation, often dismissing other beliefs or systems.

    Us vs Them Mentality: Members are encouraged to see outsiders as threats or inferior, fostering isolation.

3. Manipulative Practices

    Mind Control Techniques: Methods like indoctrination, repetition, or emotional manipulation are used to suppress critical thinking.

    Information Control: Members' access to information (external or internal) is often restricted.

    Fear and Guilt: Fear of punishment, ostracism, or eternal consequences is used to enforce compliance.

4. Exploitation of Members

    Financial Exploitation: Members may be pressured to make significant financial contributions.

Labour Exploitation: Members are often required to work for the group without fair compensation.

Psychological Exploitation: Members' emotional and psychological well-being may be manipulated to ensure loyalty.

5. Isolation from Society

Physical Isolation: Members are encouraged or forced to live apart from mainstream society.

Social Isolation: Relationships with non-members, including family and friends, are discouraged or severed.

6. Rigidity and Lack of Accountability

Strict Rules: Behaviour is tightly controlled by a rigid code of conduct.

Lack of Transparency: The group operates without external accountability or scrutiny.

Punishment for Dissent: Those who question or leave the group may face severe penalties, including shunning or public humiliation.

7. High Commitment Expectations

Total Commitment: Members are expected to prioritise the group above all else, including personal needs and relationships.

Time Demands: Participation in group activities and rituals often consumes significant time.

8. Resistance to Criticism

Defensiveness: The group reacts negatively to external criticism, often labelling critics as enemies or persecutors.

Secrecy: Practices and beliefs are often kept hidden from outsiders to avoid scrutiny.

Q6: What is the protestant movement, when did it start, and what are its main aims?

ChatGPT

The Christian Protestant movement, commonly referred to simply as Protestantism, is one of the major branches of Christianity. It originated in the early 16th century as a reaction against certain doctrines, practices, and ecclesiastical structures of the Roman Catholic Church. *Protestantism encompasses a wide range of denominations and theological perspectives, but it is united by key principles that distinguish it from Catholicism and Eastern Orthodoxy.* "Emphasis added."

Origins and Key Events

Start of the Protestant Reformation:

Date: The Protestant Reformation is considered to have begun on October 31, 1517, when Martin Luther, a German monk and theologian, famously nailed his Ninety-Five Theses to the door of the Wittenberg Castle Church. These theses criticized various church practices, particularly the sale of indulgences.

Martin Luther: Luther's actions sparked a movement that quickly spread across Europe, challenging the authority of the Pope, and calling for a return to what reformers saw as the true teachings of the Bible.

Other Key Figures:

The Reformation quickly spread throughout Europe, leading to the establishment of various Protestant denominations. Key regions of influence included Germany, Switzerland, France, England, and the Scandinavian countries.

External references

(a) "The Reformation: A History" by Diarmaid MacCulloch

(b) "Here I Stand: A Life of Martin Luther" by Roland Bainton

(c) "Institutes of the Christian Religion" by John Calvin

(d) "The Cambridge History of Christianity, Volume 6: Reform and Expansion 1500-1660"

(e) Catholic Encyclopaedia

(f) Encyclopaedia Britannica

Q7: The Sabbath is also known as the Seal of God, but why is this?

ChatGPT

The concept of the Sabbath being referred to as the "seal of God" is rooted in various theological, biblical, and symbolic interpretations. This idea is particularly prominent in some Christian denominations, such as Seventh-day Adventists, who place significant emphasis on the Sabbath. Here is a detailed explanation of why the Sabbath is considered the "seal of God":

1. Biblical Foundation

Creation Ordinance: The Sabbath is first mentioned in the Bible in Genesis 2:2-3, where God rests on the seventh day after creating the world. This day is sanctified and blessed, setting it apart as special.

Fourth Commandment: In Exodus 20:8-11, the Sabbath commandment is given as part of the Ten Commandments. It explicitly states that the seventh day is a Sabbath to the Lord, a day of rest and holiness.

2. Symbol of Covenant Relationship

Sign of the Covenant: In Exodus 31:12-17, the Sabbath is described as a sign between God and the people of Israel, signifying their unique relationship. This covenant aspect underscores the idea of the Sabbath as a distinguishing mark or seal of God's people.

Ezekiel's Emphasis: In Ezekiel 20:12, the Sabbath is again referred to as a sign between God and His people, emphasising that it serves as a reminder that God sanctifies them.

3. Theological Significance

Sanctification and Redemption: The Sabbath symbolizes not only God's creative power but also His role in sanctification and redemption. Observing the Sabbath is seen as an acknowledgment of God's authority and a commitment to living according to His will.

Rest and Restoration: The Sabbath provides a weekly opportunity for rest and spiritual rejuvenation, reflecting the ultimate rest and restoration promised in the eschatological future.

4. Seal of God in Eschatology

Revelation's Imagery: In the Book of Revelation, there are references to a seal of God placed on the foreheads of His servants (Revelation 7:3; 9:4). Some Christian groups interpret this seal symbolically as representing the observance of the Sabbath, marking those who are faithful to God's commandments.

Contrast with the Mark of the Beast: In eschatological interpretations, particularly in Adventist theology, the Sabbath is contrasted with Sunday worship, which is seen as the "Mark of the Beast." Observing the Sabbath is thus viewed as a sign of allegiance to God, while Sunday observance is seen as following human traditions.

5. Seal of Authenticity

Sign of Authenticity: A seal in ancient times was used to denote authenticity and ownership. Similarly, *the Sabbath is seen as God's seal of authenticity on His people, indicating that they belong to Him and adhere to His commandments.* "Emphasis added."

6. Spiritual Identity

Identity and Commitment: Observing the Sabbath is an outward sign of a believer's spiritual identity and commitment to God's law. It signifies a set-apart lifestyle, aligning with God's purposes and values.

Biblical Foundations

Exodus 31:13-17:

"You are to speak to the people of Israel and say, 'Above all you shall keep my Sabbaths, for this is a sign between me and you throughout your generations, that you may know that I, the Lord, sanctify you. You shall keep the Sabbath because it is holy for you... It is a sign forever between me and the people of Israel that in six days the Lord made heaven and earth, and on the seventh day he rested and was refreshed.'"

This passage explicitly states that the Sabbath is a sign between God and Israel, indicating that God is the one who sanctifies them.

Ezekiel 20:12, 20:

"Moreover, I gave them my Sabbaths, as a sign between me and them, that they might know that I am the Lord who sanctifies them... and keep my Sabbaths holy, that they may be a sign between me and you, that you may know that I am the Lord your God."

Here, the Sabbath is reaffirmed as a sign that highlights God's sanctifying power and His unique relationship with His people.

Theological Interpretation

Covenantal Sign:

The Sabbath serves as a covenantal sign, marking the special relationship between God and His people. It is a recurring, weekly reminder of their commitment to God and His sanctifying presence in their lives.

Creation and Redemption:

The Sabbath commemorates both creation and redemption. It reminds believers that God is the Creator (as seen in Exodus 20:11) and the Redeemer (Deuteronomy 5:15). By keeping the Sabbath, God's people acknowledge His sovereignty over time and their lives.

Authority:

The Sabbath underscores God's authority as the Creator who established the rhythm of six days of work followed by a day of rest. By honouring the Sabbath, believers recognise and submit to God's authority.

Identity:

The Sabbath functions as a mark of identity, signifying those who belong to God. It is a visible and practical expression of their faith and trust in God's provision and care.

Protection and Blessing:

In a symbolic sense, the Sabbath provides protection and blessing. It offers rest, renewal, and a special opportunity for communion with God, reinforcing the relationship between the Creator and His people.

Covenant Theology:

In covenant theology, the Sabbath is seen as a perpetual sign of God's covenant with His people. The "Dictionary of Biblical Imagery" discusses how the Sabbath functions as a seal in the sense of marking out God's people and their special relationship with Him.

Conclusion

The Sabbath acts as a seal for God by serving as a sign of the covenantal relationship between God and His people. It highlights God's roles as Creator and Redeemer, sanctifies His people, and sets them apart as holy. By observing the Sabbath, believers acknowledge God's authority, embrace their identity as His people, and receive His protection and blessing. This makes the Sabbath a profound spiritual seal, symbolising the unique and sacred bond between God and His followers. "Emphasis added."

External references

"Seventh-day Adventists Believe: A Biblical Exposition of Fundamental Doctrines" outlines the church's beliefs, including the significance of the Sabbath as a seal of God.

Ellen G. White's writings, particularly in "The Great Controversy" and "Testimonies for the Church," elaborate on the idea of the Sabbath as a distinguishing mark of God's true worshipers.

"New International Dictionary of Old Testament Theology and Exegesis" explores the Sabbath's role as a sign of the covenant between God and Israel.

Q8: Biblical scholar - can you show me any references to the 'forehead' in the Bible and the context in which it is used? Please use the NKJV version of the Bible.

ChatGPT

Sure, here are some references to the 'forehead' in the Bible using the New King James Version (NKJV) and their contexts:

Exodus 28:36-38 (NKJV)

Reference: "You shall also make a plate of pure gold and engrave on it, like the engraving of a signet: HOLINESS TO THE LORD. And you shall put it on a blue cord, that it may be on the turban; it shall be on the front of the turban. So, it shall be on Aaron's forehead, that Aaron may bear the iniquity of the holy things which the children of Israel hallow in all their holy gifts; and it shall always be on his forehead, that they may be accepted before the LORD."

Context: This passage details the attire of the High Priest, Aaron. The gold plate on his forehead, inscribed with "HOLINESS TO THE LORD," signifies the consecration and holiness required of the High Priest in his service, representing the bearing of Israel's iniquities.

Ezekiel 9:4 (NKJV)

Reference: "and the Lord said to him, 'Go through the midst of the city, through the midst of Jerusalem, and put a mark on the foreheads of the men who sigh and cry over all the abominations that are done within it.'"

Context: In this vision, Ezekiel sees a man clothed in linen commanded to mark the foreheads of those who lament the abominations committed in Jerusalem. This mark signifies divine protection from impending judgment.

Revelation 7:3 (NKJV)

Reference: "saying, 'Do not harm the earth, the sea, or the trees till we have sealed the servants of our God on their foreheads.'"

Context: This verse is part of the vision of the sealing of the 144,000 servants of God. The seal on their foreheads represents God's protection and their dedication to Him during the end times. Revelation 13:16 (NKJV)

Reference: "He causes all, both small and great, rich and poor, free and slave, to receive a mark on their right hand or on their foreheads,"

Context: This passage describes the actions of the second beast, compelling everyone to receive a mark on their foreheads or right hands. This mark signifies allegiance to the beast and is necessary for economic transactions.

Revelation 22:4 (NKJV)

Reference: "They shall see His face, and His name shall be on their foreheads."

Context: In the vision of the New Jerusalem, this verse describes the intimate relationship between God and His servants, who bear His name on their foreheads, symbolising belonging, and eternal fellowship with God.

Deuteronomy 6:6-8 (NKJV)

Reference: "And these words which I command you today shall be in your heart. You shall teach them diligently to your children and shall talk of them when you sit in your house, when you walk by the way, when you lie down, and when you rise up. You shall bind them as a sign on your hand, and they shall be as frontlets between your eyes."

Context: These verses emphasise the importance of keeping God's commandments constantly in mind and heart, symbolized by binding them on the hands and foreheads. This represents an ever-present reminder to live according to God's laws. These references highlight the symbolic importance of the forehead in biblical texts, often relating to identity, protection, dedication, and the contrast between divine and opposing spiritual allegiances.

External references:

The Anchor Yale Bible Dictionary, Vol. 2, p. 481-483, discusses the cultural and symbolic significance of the forehead in ancient Near Eastern contexts, which sheds light on its usage in biblical literature.

Q9: Thank you. I noticed the phrase, 'second beast'. In Biblical prophecy, what is a beast, and who is the first and second beast, can you be more specific?

ChatGPT

In Biblical prophecy, particularly in the Book of Revelation, "beasts" are symbolic representations of political or religious powers that oppose God and His people. They are typically described in vivid, allegorical language to convey their characteristics and actions. The first and second beasts are specifically mentioned in Revelation 13.

The First Beast (Revelation 13:1-10, NKJV)

Reference: "Then I stood on the sand of the sea. And I saw a beast rising up out of the sea, having seven heads and ten horns, and on his horns ten crowns, and on his heads a blasphemous name. Now the beast which I saw was like a leopard, his feet were like the feet of a bear, and his mouth like the mouth of a lion. The dragon gave him his power, his throne, and great authority."

Description and Context: The first beast emerges from the sea, which often symbolizes chaotic, ungovernable masses of humanity. This beast has ten horns and seven heads, symbolising a confederation of powerful kingdoms or rulers. The beast resembles a leopard, with feet like a bear's and a mouth like a lion's, combining traits of various powerful animals described in Daniel's visions (Daniel 7). The dragon (Satan) gives the beast its power and authority, indicating that it operates with satanic influence and opposition to God. The first beast is often interpreted as representing a powerful, persecuting empire or political power that blasphemes against God and oppresses His people.

The Second Beast (Revelation 13:11-18, NKJV)

Reference: "Then I saw another beast coming up out of the earth, and he had two horns like a lamb and spoke like a dragon. And he exercises all the authority of the first beast in his presence and causes the earth and those who dwell in it to worship the first beast, whose deadly wound was healed. He performs great signs, so that he even makes fire come down from heaven on the earth in the sight of men. And he deceives those who dwell on the earth by those signs which he was granted to do in the sight of the beast, telling those who dwell on the earth to make an image to the beast who was wounded by the sword and lived."

Description and Context: The second beast rises from the earth, symbolising a more stable, organised power compared to the chaotic sea. It has two horns like a lamb but speaks like a dragon, indicating a deceptive nature—it appears gentle and harmless but is aligned with satanic forces. This beast exercises the authority of the first beast and promotes worship of the first beast, whose "deadly wound was healed," signifying a revival of a defeated power. The second beast performs miraculous signs to deceive people, including making fire come down from heaven. It instructs people to create an image of the first beast and mandates worship of this image, enforcing its decrees with economic control, symbolized by the infamous "Mark of the Beast" (Revelation 13:16-17).

Symbolism and Interpretation

First Beast: Generally interpreted as a representation of a powerful, blasphemous political empire that opposes God's kingdom. Historically, some scholars and theologians have identified it with the Roman Empire, due to its persecutory practices against early Christians. Others see it as a future global empire with similar characteristics.

Second Beast: Often seen as a false prophet or religious authority that supports the first beast, deceiving people into worshiping the first beast. This beast's ability to perform miracles and enforce economic control signifies a compelling, influential religious or ideological power that complements the political power of the first beast.

In summary, the beasts in Revelation symbolize powerful entities—political and religious—that work in opposition to God, deceiving and persecuting His people. The first beast represents a political empire, while the second beast represents a supportive religious or ideological authority, both operating under satanic influence.

External references:

Craig R. Koester, "Revelation": Koester provides a detailed analysis of the historical context, associating the first beast with Roman imperial power.

Richard Bauckham, "The Theology of the Book of Revelation": Bauckham explores how the imagery connects to Roman political and religious practices.

Tim LaHaye "Revelation Unveiled": LaHaye discusses the first beast in the context of end-time prophecy, identifying it as the Antichrist.

Iain M. Duguid, "A Reformation Commentary on Scripture: Revelation": This commentary includes historicist interpretations from Reformation theologians.

Serena A. Sugano, "The Book of Revelation and Early Jewish Textual Culture": Sugano examines the second beast in the context of Roman religious practices.

Craig R. Koester, "Revelation and the End of All Things": Koester discusses the role of the second beast in promoting false worship.

Martin Luther, "The Babylonian Captivity of the Church": Luther's critique of the Papacy includes references to Revelation.

John Calvin, "Institutes of the Christian Religion": Calvin offers critiques of the Roman Catholic Church, connecting it to the imagery of Revelation.

Hank Hanegraaff, "The Apocalypse Code": Hanegraaff examines various futurist interpretations, including those involving the second beast.

Q10: That is good, but are you able to identify the religious or political powers behind these two Beasts?

ChatGPT

The identification of the two beasts in Revelation 13 has been a subject of extensive interpretation and debate among scholars, theologians, and various religious traditions. Different interpretations exist, often influenced by historical, theological, and eschatological perspectives. Here are some of the prominent views regarding the religious and political powers behind the two beasts:

Historicist Interpretation

The historicist perspective interprets the beasts as symbols of historical powers that have manifested throughout church history.

First Beast (Political Power):

Roman Empire: Many historicists identify the first beast with the Roman Empire, particularly its later phase as the Holy Roman Empire. This interpretation sees the beast as representing the political and military power that persecuted Christians and opposed the spread of the Gospel.

Papacy: Some also see the first beast as symbolising the papal system, particularly during periods when the Roman Catholic Church held significant political power and influence over European kings and emperors.

Second Beast (Religious Power):

Roman Catholic Church/False Prophet: The second beast is often identified with the religious authority of the Papacy, seen as promoting the worship of the first beast (the political power). This interpretation views the papal system as having a deceptive, controlling influence over religious and secular matters, performing "miracles" to validate its authority.

Futurist Interpretation

The futurist perspective sees the beasts as representing future entities that will emerge during the end times.

First Beast (Political Power):

Future Global Empire/Antichrist: Futurists often identify the first beast with a future global political leader or empire, sometimes called the Antichrist. This figure is seen as a world dictator who will oppose God and persecute believers during a period of great tribulation.

Second Beast (Religious Power):

False Prophet: The second beast is identified as a future religious leader who will support the Antichrist, performing miracles and deceiving people into worshiping the first beast. This false prophet will have significant religious influence and promote the Antichrist's agenda.

Idealist Interpretation.

Conclusion

The specific identification of the religious or political powers behind the two beasts varies significantly depending on one's interpretive framework. Each perspective provides a different lens through which to understand these symbolic entities in the Book of Revelation.

External references:

"Revelation" by Craig R. Koester: This commentary provides an in-depth analysis of the historical context of Revelation, discussing the Roman Empire's role.

"The Theology of the Book of Revelation" by Richard Bauckham: Bauckham explores how the imagery of the Beast connects to Roman imperial power.

"Revelation: Four Views: A Parallel Commentary" edited by Steve Gregg: This book presents different interpretative perspectives, including futurist views.

"The Book of Revelation" by Robert H. Mounce: Mounce provides a detailed analysis of the text from a futurist perspective.

"A Reformation Commentary on Scripture: Revelation" edited by Iain M. Duguid: This commentary includes historicist interpretations from Reformation theologians.

"The Book of Revelation and Early Jewish Textual Culture" by Serena A. Sugano: Sugano examines the second Beast in the context of Roman religious practices.

"Revelation and the End of All Things" by Craig R. Koester: Koester discusses the second Beast's role in promoting false worship.

"The Babylonian Captivity of the Church" by Martin Luther: Luther explicitly discusses his views on the Papacy.

"Institutes of the Christian Religion" by John Calvin: Calvin offers critiques of the Roman Catholic Church, connecting it to the imagery of Revelation.

"The Apocalypse Code" by Hank Hanegraaff: Hanegraaff

examines various futurist interpretations, including those involving the second Beast.

"Revelation Unveiled" by Tim LaHaye: LaHaye, a prominent futurist, discusses the role of the second Beast in end-time prophecy.

Q11: You have said that from a historicist position the Roman Catholic Church has been identified as the second beast and will seek to enforce the change in sacredness from Saturday to Sunday, but what have they said about this change?

ChatGPT

The Roman Catholic Church has historically acknowledged its role in the change of the Sabbath observance from Saturday to Sunday. Here are a few notable points and statements made by Catholic authorities regarding this change:

Council of Laodicea (A.D. 363-364):

The Council of Laodicea was one of the early instances where the Church addressed the observance of the Sabbath. Canon 29 of this council states:

"Christians shall not Judaize and be idle on Saturday but shall work on that day; but the Lord's day they shall especially honour, and, as being Christians, shall, if possible, do no work on that day. If, however, they are found Judaizing, they shall be shut out from Christ."

The Catechism of the Catholic Church:

The modern Catechism of the Catholic Church discusses the observance of Sunday instead of the traditional Sabbath (Saturday):

"The Church celebrates the day of Christ's Resurrection on the 'eighth day,' Sunday, which is rightly called the Lord's Day (cf. SC 106)."

Cardinal James Gibbons (late 19th and early 20th century):

In his book "The Faith of Our Fathers" (1876), Cardinal Gibbons wrote:

"You may read the Bible from Genesis to Revelation, and you will not find a single line authorising the sanctification of Sunday. The Scriptures enforce the religious observance of Saturday, a day which we never sanctify."

The Catholic Mirror (1893):

The official organ of Cardinal Gibbons, The Catholic Mirror, published a series of articles in 1893 addressing the change of the Sabbath:

"Reason and common sense demand the acceptance of one or the other of these alternatives: Either Protestantism and the keeping holy of Saturday, or Catholicity and the keeping holy of Sunday. Compromise is impossible."

The Convert's Catechism of Catholic Doctrine (1946):

Written by Peter Geiermann, this catechism states:

"Q. Which is the Sabbath day?

A. Saturday is the Sabbath day.

Q. Why do we observe Sunday instead of Saturday?

A. We observe Sunday instead of Saturday because the Catholic Church transferred the solemnity from Saturday to Sunday."

These references highlight the Catholic Church's acknowledgment of its role in changing the day of worship from Saturday to Sunday, emphasising its authority to make such changes in observance. This shift is seen as a significant demonstration of the Church's authority, which they claim to exercise in matters of doctrine and practice.

Commentary: I reaffirm my assertion that the sacredness of the Sabbath has not been transferred to Sunday or any other day. Only God holds the authority to make such a change, and His original design for the Sabbath is perfect, unalterable, and established for eternity.

External references:

Catholic Encyclopaedia:

- The Catholic Encyclopaedia acknowledges that the Church transferred the solemnity from Saturday to Sunday, which is seen as an exercise of the Church's authority. The Encyclopaedia states, "The Church, after changing the day of rest from the Jewish Sabbath, or seventh day of the week, to the first, made the Third Commandment refer to Sunday as the day to be kept holy as the Lord's Day" (Fatima Centre).

National Catholic Register:

- The National Catholic Register explains that Sunday is distinct from the Jewish Sabbath and that for Christians, its ceremonial observance replaces that of the Sabbath. The article mentions, "Sunday thus fulfils what the Sabbath pointed toward" and indicates that this change was an established practice by the early Church, referencing the observance of "the Lord's day" as early as the first century (National Catholic Register).

Catholic Answers:

- In an article by Catholic Answers, it is noted that the observance of Sunday over the Jewish Sabbath is rooted in the resurrection of Jesus Christ, which took place on a Sunday. The article explains that early Christians began to observe Sunday as a day of worship and rest, distinguishing it from the traditional

Jewish Sabbath. It asserts that the Church, under the guidance of the Holy Spirit, has the authority to set liturgical practices for Christians (Catholic Answers).

- Neutral view on the Beast of Revelation: (Wikipedia on Beast of Revelation)

Q12: Good morning, Bible scholar. Will it be the first and second beasts that will instigate the Mark of the Beast, and what is their intention for that?

ChatGPT

Good morning! In the Book of Revelation, the "Mark of the Beast" is a significant element in the eschatological narrative. The instigation of this mark is indeed associated with the first and second beasts described in Revelation 13. Let us break this down with references from the text.

The First Beast

The first beast is introduced in Revelation 13:1-10. This beast rises out of the sea, having ten horns and seven heads, with ten crowns on its horns and blasphemous names on its heads. It is described as a composite of a leopard, bear, and lion, which symbolizes a powerful and terrifying entity.

The Second Beast

The second beast appears in Revelation 13:11-18. This beast rises out of the earth, having two horns like a lamb but speaking like a dragon. This second beast is also known as the false prophet, as indicated later in Revelation 16:13, 19:20, and 20:10.

Role in Instituting the Mark

Revelation 13:16-17 specifically describes how the second beast causes people to receive the mark:

"It also forced all people, great and small, rich and poor, free and slave, to receive a mark on their right hands or on their foreheads, so that they could not buy or sell unless they had the mark, which is the name of the beast or the number of its name."

From this passage, we see that the second beast enforces the reception of the mark. The first beast, which represents a powerful political or worldly authority, is the one whose mark is given. The second beast, often interpreted as a religious or deceptive authority, compels the population to worship the first beast and receive its mark. "Emphasis added."

Intention Behind the Mark

The intention behind the Mark of the Beast can be inferred from the surrounding context and the roles of the beasts:

Control and Allegiance: The mark signifies allegiance to the first beast and ensures control over economic activities (buying and selling). This is a means to consolidate power and ensure that only those loyal to the beast can participate in society. "Emphasis added."

Blasphemy and Defiance Against God: The mark is also a symbol of defiance against God. Revelation 13:6 mentions the first beast blaspheming God's name, His dwelling, and those who dwell in heaven. The mark represents a rejection of God's authority in favour of the beast's dominion.

Deception and Idolatry: The second beast performs great signs and deceives those who dwell on the earth (Revelation 13:13-14), compelling them to make an image of the first beast and worship it. The mark thus also serves to perpetuate this deception and idolatry.

Conclusion

In summary, the Mark of the Beast is instigated by the second beast to enforce worship and allegiance to the first beast, consolidating economic and religious control while symbolising rebellion against God. The intention is multifaceted, aiming to dominate, deceive, and lead people away from God and towards the worship of the beast. "Emphasis added."

External references:

Bible Gateway - Revelation 13:1-10
Describes the first beast's rise and its blasphemous authority.

Bible Gateway - Revelation 13:11-18
Details the second beast's role in enforcing the Mark of the Beast.

GotQuestions.org - What is the Mark of the Beast?
Explains the significance and implications of the mark.

Enduring Word - Revelation 13 Commentary
Provides a detailed commentary on Revelation 13, including the roles of the first and second beasts.

Catholic Answers - The Two Beasts of Revelation 13
These sources provide a comprehensive view of the roles and intentions of the first and second beasts in enforcing the Mark of the Beast, as well as the broader theological and prophetic implications.

Q13: Will I know that I have the Mark of the Beast?

ChatGPT

According to the Book of Revelation, receiving the mark of the Beast is a conscious decision, implying that individuals will be aware of their choice. "Emphasis added."

Here are some key points that suggest people will know if they have received the mark:

Conscious Decision and Worship

Explicit Choice of Worship: Revelation 13:15-17 highlights that the mark is linked to the worship of the Beast and its image. This worship is a deliberate act, indicating that individuals will be consciously choosing to align themselves with the Beast's authority. "Emphasis added."

"The second beast was given power to give breath to the image of the first beast, so that the image could speak and cause all who refused to worship the image to be killed. It also forced all people, great and small, rich and poor, free and slave, to receive a mark on their right hands or on their foreheads, so that they could not buy or sell unless they had the mark, which is the name of the beast or the number of its name."

Economic and Social Consequences: The mark is necessary for buying and selling, which would be a significant and noticeable change in daily life. People will recognise the economic and social implications of receiving or refusing the mark.

The Nature of the Mark

Foreheads and Right Hands: The mark is placed on the right hand or the forehead (Revelation 13:16), which are visible and intentional locations. This suggests an overt and acknowledged decision rather than something that can be received unknowingly. "Emphasis added."

Biblical Warnings and Consequences

Warnings from Scripture: Revelation 14:9-11 provides a stern warning about the consequences of receiving the mark, indicating that individuals are being warned about the seriousness of this act.

"A third angel followed them and said in a loud voice: 'If anyone worships the beast and its image and receives its mark on their forehead or on their hand, they, too, will drink the wine of God's fury, which has been poured full strength into the cup of his wrath. They will be tormented with burning sulphur in the presence of the holy angels and of the Lamb. And the smoke of their torment will rise for ever and ever. There will be no rest day or night for those who worship the beast and its image, or for anyone who receives the mark of its name.'" This passage indicates that the act of receiving the mark is serious and carries eternal consequences, reinforcing the idea that it is a known and conscious decision.

Conclusion

Based on these points, the Bible presents the Mark of the Beast as something individuals will knowingly accept. The decision to receive the mark is associated with worshiping the Beast and entails significant social and economic changes that will make the mark's presence and implications evident.

External References

1. The Anchor Yale Bible Dictionary (Vol. 4, p. 126): This dictionary discusses the "Mark of the Beast" in the context of apocalyptic literature and its symbolic meaning related to loyalty and worship.
2. "The Mark of the Beast" by Robert H. Mounce: Mounce, in his commentary on Revelation, explores the historical and theological implications of the mark, connecting it to the Roman Empire's demand for emperor worship and the broader theme of spiritual allegiance.
3. "Apocalypse: A Brief History" by Martha Himmelfarb: Himmelfarb examines the development of apocalyptic thought and the symbolic nature of the mark, emphasising its role in

distinguishing between those loyal to God and those loyal to worldly powers.

4. "Revelation: Four Views - A Parallel Commentary" edited by Steve Gregg:

This commentary provides multiple interpretations of the Mark of the Beast, including preterist, historicist, futurist, and idealist perspectives, offering a comprehensive understanding of its significance in different eschatological frameworks.

Q14: What is the significance of receiving the Mark of the Beast in my hand?

ChatGPT

The concept of receiving the "Mark of the Beast" in the hand (or on the forehead) is found in the Book of Revelation, specifically in Revelation 13. This mark is a symbol of allegiance to the beast, a figure representing opposition to God and His followers. Understanding the significance of this mark involves exploring its biblical context and theological implications.

Receiving the mark is tied to economic transactions, as it is stated that no one can buy or sell without it. This implies a system where economic survival is contingent upon submission to the beast's authority, representing control over daily life and necessities.

The hand often represents actions and deeds, while the forehead represents thoughts and beliefs. Receiving the mark on the hand or forehead suggests a comprehensive submission to the beast, encompassing both behaviour (actions) and mindset (beliefs).

External References

1. The Anchor Yale Bible Dictionary (Vol. 4, p. 126)

This reference discusses the "Mark of the Beast" in the context of apocalyptic literature and its symbolic meaning related to loyalty and worship, drawing parallels with other ancient Near Eastern practices of marking slaves or soldiers to signify ownership or allegiance.

2. "Revelation" by G.K. Beale
   Beale's commentary explores the historical and theological implications of the mark, analysing how it relates to Roman imperial cult practices where loyalty to the emperor was often enforced.

3. "The Book of Revelation: A Commentary on the Greek Text" by G.K. Beale
   This detailed commentary provides in-depth analysis on the symbolism of the mark, connecting it to historical contexts and theological interpretations.

4. "The Theology of the Book of Revelation" by Richard Bauckham.
   The author examines the broader theological themes in Revelation, including the Mark of the Beast, and how it fits into the overall message of the book.

5. "Apocalypse: A Brief History" by Martha Himmelfarb
   Himmelfarb's work provides historical context to apocalyptic literature and examines the development of the concept of the mark, emphasising its role in distinguishing between those loyal to God and those loyal to worldly powers.

Q15: What is the Image of the Beast?

ChatGPT

In Revelation 14:9, the "image of the beast" is a significant symbol within the apocalyptic vision. Here is the verse for context:

"And the third angel followed them, saying with a loud voice, 'If any man worships the beast and his image, and receive his mark in his forehead, or in his hand,'"

The "image of the beast" refers to an object or representation associated with the beast, which in turn symbolizes a powerful and malevolent entity that opposes God and leads people into idolatry and deception. The image is meant to be worshipped by people, and this act of worship signifies their allegiance to the beast rather than to God.

Interpretations of the image of the beast vary among scholars and religious traditions, but it is commonly understood as a representation of the false systems, ideologies, or authorities that demand ultimate loyalty and worship in opposition to God. In a broader sense, it can be seen as a symbol of idolatry and the coercive power of evil forces in the world.

External References

1. "The Book of Revelation: A Commentary on the Greek Text" by G.K. Beale

Beale's commentary offers a comprehensive analysis of the image of the beast, discussing its historical context and theological implications. He explores how the image functions as a symbol of idolatry and false worship, drawing parallels to Roman imperial cult practices.

2. "The Theology of the Book of Revelation" by Richard Bauckham

Bauckham examines the broader theological themes in Revelation, including the image of the beast. He discusses how the image represents a counterfeit of true worship and reflects the totalitarian nature of the beast's rule.

3. "Revelation" by Craig S. Keener

Keener provides an accessible yet scholarly examination of Revelation, including detailed discussions on the image of the beast. He contextualizes the image within the first-century Roman world and explores its significance for contemporary readers.

4. "The Apocalypse of John: A Commentary" by R.H. Charles

Charles' classic commentary delves into the symbolism of the image of the beast, providing historical insights and interpretations from early Christian thought.

5. "The New International Commentary on the New Testament: The Book of Revelation" by Robert H. Mounce

Mounce's commentary offers a thorough exegesis of the image of the beast, exploring its role in the narrative of Revelation and its implications for understanding the conflict between good and evil.

Q16: Has the United States been widely identified as playing any role in end time prophecy, particularly around enforcement of worship?

ChatGPT

Yes, within certain Christian eschatological frameworks, particularly among some Protestant and evangelical groups, the United States has been widely identified as playing a role in end-time prophecy, especially regarding the enforcement of worship. Here are some key points related to this interpretation:

1. Historicist Perspective

The Second Beast of Revelation 13

Description: The second beast in Revelation 13:11-17 is described as having "two horns like a lamb but speaking like a dragon."

Interpretation: Many historicist interpreters, particularly within Seventh-day Adventism, identify this beast as representing the United States. They see the lamb-like horns as symbols of the country's principles of civil and religious liberty, while the dragon-like voice signifies a future shift towards coercive power.

Role in Worship Enforcement: This perspective holds that the United States will play a pivotal role in enforcing religious observance, specifically Sunday worship, aligning with the authority of the first beast, commonly associated with the Roman Catholic Church.

Enforcement of Sunday Worship

Sunday Laws: The historicist view predicts that the United States will enact and enforce laws mandating Sunday worship, which they see as contrary to the biblical Sabbath (Saturday).

Persecution: Those who observe the Sabbath on Saturday, such as Seventh-day Adventists, are believed to face persecution for their refusal to comply with these Sunday laws.

The Sunday Law in the Past

Regarding the national Sunday Law, many are under the impression that this is something new that will be introduced in the future. Think again! The fact is, if you are more than 30 years old, you have lived under Sunday trading restrictions at some time in your life. Here is a summary of the situation in the UK.

1. Sunday trading laws in the UK were reformed by the Sunday Trading Act 1994, which came into effect on 26 August 1994. Before this, the restrictions on Sunday trading were in place primarily due

to religious and cultural reasons, aimed at preserving Sunday as a day of rest and worship.

2. Sunday Observance Act 1677: One of the earliest pieces of legislation that restricted Sunday trading was the Sunday Observance Act 1677. It prohibited many commercial activities on Sundays to ensure that people could attend church and observe the day of rest.

Reasons for Restrictions

- Religious Reasons: The primary reason for the restrictions was to allow people to observe Sunday as a religious day, attend church services, and spend time with family.
- Social Reasons: There was also a social aspect to these laws, aiming to provide a common day off for workers, enabling families to spend time together.
- Cultural Tradition: The tradition of a Sunday rest day was deeply ingrained in British culture, and the laws reflected the societal norms and values of the time.

The UK was not alone in this practice because, there was a time in the United States when it was prohibited to buy and sell on Sundays. These restrictions were known as "blue laws", designed to enforce religious standards, particularly the observance of Sunday as a day of worship and rest. These laws restricted or prohibited certain activities, including commercial transactions, on Sundays.

Blue laws have a long history in the United States, dating back to colonial times. They originated in the 17th century with the Puritans in New England. For instance, the Massachusetts Bay Colony enacted blue laws in 1651, which included prohibitions on Sunday activities. Some blue laws, particularly those concerning the sale of alcohol on Sundays, persisted in various states into the 2000s.

What I will say about the 're-introduction' of the Sunday Law is that enforcement will be ramped up. It won't just be that Sunday is official, but you can still worship on your preferred day. No, worship will become mandated on Sunday, with serious consequences for non-compliance.

3. Dispensationalist Perspective
   Support for Israel
   End-Time Events: In dispensationalist eschatology, the United States is often seen as playing a supportive role for Israel, which is central to many end-time prophecies.

   Global Influence: While not always specifying worship enforcement, dispensationalists recognise the United States as a significant global power influencing end-time events, particularly through its political and military support for Israel.

4. General Evangelical Views
   Moral Decline and Apostasy
   Signs of the Times: Many evangelicals interpret the perceived moral and spiritual decline in the United States as a sign of the approaching end times. This decline is viewed as part of a larger pattern of global apostasy predicted in the Bible.

   Role in Global Events
   Economic and Political Actions: The United States' actions on the global stage are often seen as shaping end-time events. This includes international conflicts, economic policies, and diplomatic efforts that align with biblical prophecies.

5. Other Interpretations
   Babylon the Great

Alternative Identification: Some interpretations suggest that the United States could be identified with "Babylon the Great" in Revelation 17-18, symbolising a powerful, influential nation facing divine judgment. This view is less common but present in some prophetic circles.

Modern Israel's Protector

Dispensationalist View: In line with dispensationalist thought, the U.S. is seen as a protector of modern Israel, significant for fulfilling end-time prophecies related to Israel's restoration and protection.

Conclusion

The identification of the United States in end-time prophecy, particularly around the enforcement of worship, is a common theme in certain Christian eschatological interpretations. Historicist views, especially within Seventh-day Adventism, see the U.S. as the second beast of Revelation 13, playing a coercive role in enforcing Sunday worship. Dispensationalist and many evangelical perspectives emphasize the U.S. as a major global power influencing end-time events, often focusing on its support for Israel. These interpretations reflect the diverse ways in which biblical prophecy is understood and applied to contemporary geopolitics.

External References

1. "The Great Controversy" by Ellen G. White

This seminal work by one of the founders of the Seventh-day Adventist Church provides a detailed exposition of the Adventist interpretation of prophecy, including the role of the United States in end-time events. White argues that the U.S. will play a crucial role in enforcing religious conformity and Sunday worship, which she views as contrary to the biblical Sabbath.

2. "Revelation: Four Views – A Parallel Commentary" edited by Steve Gregg

This commentary provides multiple interpretations of Revelation, including historicist, preterist, futurist, and idealist views. It offers insights into how different Christian traditions have interpreted the prophetic texts, including views on the United States' potential role.

3. "The Mark of the Beast" by John H. Ogwyn

This book discusses various interpretations of the Mark of the Beast and the entities involved in enforcing it. Ogwyn's work reflects a broader evangelical perspective that often links contemporary political and religious developments to prophetic fulfilment.

4. "The United States in Prophecy" by Herbert W. Armstrong

Armstrong, founder of the Worldwide Church of God, wrote extensively on the role of the United States in biblical prophecy. His views are distinct but still place significant emphasis on the U.S. as a key player in end-time events.

Q17: As a revered neurosurgeon, please explain in simple terms what happens in my forehead.

ChatGPT

Sure! Let us talk about what happens in the forehead in simple terms.

Your Forehead and the Brain

Your forehead covers a part of the brain called the frontal lobes. The frontal lobes are crucial for many essential functions:

Thinking and Planning: The frontal lobes help you make decisions, solve problems, and plan your actions. When you are thinking about what to do next or making a choice, this part of your brain is at work.

Personality and Behaviour: Your personality traits, like how you react to different situations and interact with others, are influenced by the frontal lobes. They help control your behaviour and emotions.

Movement: The part of the frontal lobes called the motor cortex helps control your voluntary movements. For example, when you decide to move your hand, the motor cortex sends signals to your muscles to make that movement happen.

Speech and Language: There is a specific area in the frontal lobe called Broca's area that is important for speech production. It helps you form the words you want to say.

External References

1. "Principles of Neural Science" by Eric Kandel, James Schwartz, and Thomas Jessell

   This comprehensive textbook provides detailed information about the functions of different brain regions, including the frontal lobe and prefrontal cortex.

2. Mayo Clinic: Frontal Lobe Function

   The Mayo Clinic offers accessible explanations of the various functions of the frontal lobe and how they affect behaviour and cognitive processes. Mayo Clinic - Frontal Lobe

3.   National Institute of Neurological Disorders and Stroke (NINDS)

NINDS provides information on neurological functions and disorders, including those affecting the frontal lobe. NINDS - Frontal Lobe

Q18: What is the Seal of God and where can I find Biblical references?

The Seal of God represents His mark of ownership, approval, and protection over His faithful followers. It signifies allegiance to God and acceptance of His authority. Biblically, the seal of God is closely associated with obedience to His law, particularly the observance of the Sabbath, which is a sign of His covenant with His people.

Key Biblical References:

1.   The Seal as a Mark of God's Ownership

Ezekiel 20:12 (NKJV): "Moreover I also gave them My Sabbaths, to be a sign between them and Me, that they might know that I am the Lord who sanctifies them."

The Sabbath is identified as a sign of God's sanctifying power and covenant relationship.

Ezekiel 20:20 (NKJV): "Hallow My Sabbaths, and they will be a sign between Me and you, that you may know that I am the Lord your God."

Observance of the Sabbath is a distinguishing mark of God's people.

2.   The Seal as a Mark of Protection

Revelation 7:2–3 (NKJV): "Then I saw another angel ascending from the east, having the seal of the living God. And he cried with a loud voice to the four angels to whom it was granted to harm the earth and the sea, saying, 'Do not harm the earth, the sea, or the trees till we have sealed the servants of our God on their foreheads.'"

The seal is placed on the foreheads of God's faithful, symbolising their commitment and protection during the final judgement.

3. God's Law and the Seal

Isaiah 8:16 (NKJV): "Bind up the testimony, seal the law among my disciples."

The seal relates to God's law, signifying adherence to His commandments.

Exodus 31:16–17 (NKJV): "Therefore the children of Israel shall keep the Sabbath, to observe the Sabbath throughout their generations as a perpetual covenant. It is a sign between Me and the children of Israel forever."

The Sabbath is described as a perpetual sign of God's authority as Creator. Several respected theologians, Bible scholars, and commentaries support the interpretation of the Fourth Commandment as God's seal. Here are some external references that reinforce this understanding:

1. Theological Commentary

Adam Clarke's Commentary on the Bible (Exodus 20:8–11)

Clarke highlights the Sabbath's role as a perpetual sign of God's authority as Creator and Sustainer. He emphasizes that the Sabbath is a recognition of God's sovereign work in creation.

Matthew Henry's Commentary (Exodus 20)

Henry connects the Sabbath to God's identity and His relationship with His people, recognizing it as a memorial of creation and a mark of His covenant.

Scholars like Kenneth A. Kitchen have noted that ancient seals in biblical times included three elements: name, title, and territory. The Fourth Commandment follows this structure, making it a theological seal reflecting God's kingship and covenant.

The Fourth Commandment is found in Exodus 20:8–11 (NKJV):

"Remember the Sabbath day, to keep it holy. Six days you shall labour and do all your work, but the seventh day is the Sabbath of the Lord your God. In it you shall do no work: you, nor your son, nor your daughter, nor your male servant, nor your female servant, nor your cattle, nor your stranger who is within your gates. For in six days the Lord made the heavens and the earth, the sea, and all that is in them, and rested the seventh day. Therefore, the Lord blessed the Sabbath day and hallowed it."

This commandment emphasises the sanctity of the Sabbath, its connection to creation, and the divine blessing placed upon it.

The sovereign's name is the Lord God, Title: Creator, Territory: heaven and earth.

Q19: How do I receive the Seal of God in my forehead?

ChatGPT

The "seal of God" mentioned in the Book of Revelation represents a mark of protection and ownership by God, distinguishing His faithful followers from those who follow the Beast. This seal is described in several passages within the context of end-times events.

Biblical References

Revelation 7:2-4: This passage describes the sealing of the 144,000 servants of God on their foreheads:

"Then I saw another angel coming up from the east, having the seal of the living God. He called out in a loud voice to the four angels who had been given power to harm the land and the sea: 'Do not harm the land or the sea or the trees until we put a seal on the foreheads of the servants of our God.' Then I heard the number of those who were sealed: 144,000 from all the tribes of Israel."

This seal signifies protection from God's coming judgments and identifies these individuals as belonging to Him.

Revelation 9:4: During the fifth trumpet judgment, those with the seal of God are protected from harm:

"They were told not to harm the grass of the earth or any plant or tree, but only those people who did not have the seal of God on their foreheads."

Here, the seal provides protection from the torment inflicted by the locust-like creatures released during this judgment.

Revelation 14:1: This verse shows the Lamb (Jesus) standing on Mount Zion with the 144,000 who have His name and His Father's name written on their foreheads:

"Then I looked, and there before me was the Lamb, standing on Mount Zion, and with him 144,000 who had his name and his Father's name written on their foreheads."

The seal here is explicitly described as containing the name of the Lamb and the Father, symbolising their belonging and loyalty to God.

Symbolism and Significance

The seal of God serves several purposes:

Ownership and Loyalty: The seal signifies that those who receive it belong to God. It marks them as His faithful servants, set apart from those who follow the Beast.

Protection: The seal protects God's people from certain judgments and calamities that befall the rest of the world during the end times. This is particularly evident in the passages from Revelation 7 and 9.

Identity and Holiness: By bearing the name of God and the Lamb, the seal also represents the identity and holiness of God's people. It signifies their commitment to God's covenant and their separation from the corrupt world system represented by the Beast.

Conclusion

The seal of God on the forehead of believers is a powerful symbol of divine protection, ownership, and identity. It marks them as God's own, providing assurance of His presence and favour during the tumultuous events of the end times. This seal distinguishes the faithful followers of God from those who receive the Mark of the Beast, highlighting their loyalty and dedication to God's kingdom.

External References

1.   "The Great Controversy" by Ellen G. White

This book, written by one of the founders of the Seventh-day Adventist Church, discusses in detail the concept of the Seal of God, particularly in the context of end-time prophecy and the observance of the Sabbath.

2.   "Revelation: Four Views – A Parallel Commentary" edited by Steve Gregg

This commentary offers multiple interpretations of the Book of Revelation, including the concept of the Seal of God, from historicist, preterist, futurist, and idealist perspectives.

3. "The Mark of the Beast" by John H. Ogwyn

This book explores the theological implications of the seal and the Mark of the Beast, providing a broader context for understanding end-time prophecies.

4. "The Seal of God" by Arthur L. White

Arthur L. White's work focuses specifically on the Biblical and theological understanding of the Seal of God, emphasising its importance in Christian eschatology.

Q20: Will I receive the seal of God through choice, or will it be a physical application on the forehead?

ChatGPT

The concept of the "seal of God" is often discussed within Christian eschatology, particularly in relation to the Book of Revelation in the New Testament. Interpretations of what this seal represents and how it is received can vary among different Christian denominations and theological perspectives.

Spiritual Interpretation: Many Christian theologians and denominations interpret the seal of God as a symbolic or spiritual mark rather than a physical one. According to this view, the seal signifies being chosen or protected by God and is received through faith, repentance, and adherence to God's commandments. This seal is often associated with the Holy Spirit's indwelling presence in believers, marking them as God's own.

Physical Interpretation: Some groups or interpretations take the idea of a physical mark more literally. However, this perspective is less common and is not the mainstream view among most Christian traditions. Those who hold to a more literal interpretation might see it as an actual mark or sign placed on the forehead, but this is not widely accepted.

Choice and Faith: *Regardless of whether the seal is viewed as spiritual or physical, the concept of choice is crucial in Christian theology. Receiving the seal of God is typically understood as involving a personal decision to follow God, accept Jesus Christ, and live according to biblical teachings. This decision and commitment are seen as key factors in being marked as one of God's people.* "Emphasis added."

In summary, while interpretations vary, the majority view within Christianity is that the seal of God is a spiritual mark received through faith and choice rather than a physical application on the forehead. This seal signifies a believer's relationship with God and their commitment to living a life in accordance with His will.

External References

1. "The Great Controversy" by Ellen G. White:

Ellen G. White discusses the Seal of God extensively, emphasising its spiritual nature and the importance of personal choice in aligning with God's commandments, particularly the observance of the Sabbath.

2. "Revelation: Four Views – A Parallel Commentary" edited by Steve Gregg:

This commentary provides multiple interpretations of the Book of Revelation, offering insights into how different Christian traditions understand the Seal of God as a spiritual rather than physical mark.

3. "The Mark of the Beast" by John H. Ogwyn:

Ogwyn explores the theological implications of both the Mark of the Beast and the Seal of God, highlighting the symbolic nature of these marks and the importance of spiritual allegiance and choice.

4. "The Seal of God" by Arthur L. White:

This work delves into the biblical and theological understanding of the Seal of God, emphasising the spiritual transformation and commitment required to receive the seal.

Conclusion

I want to stress that: worshipping on Sunday today, does not mean that you have the Mark of the Beast. For that to happen, there must be an enforceable law declaring Sunday as the mandated day of worship. Not only that; you will know the truth of the biblical Sabbath, but for the sake of self-preservation, you will choose to worship on Sunday instead of Saturday. Furthermore, you will support this rebellious regime with your efforts and means. This choice cannot be underestimated—you will not be able to buy or sell and may not even be able to secure gainful employment if you do not comply. This is where your faith will be tested to the limit.

The Mark of the Beast and the Seal of God are both indicative of the choices you will make regarding whom you will worship. The first angel of (Revelation 14:6) encourages us to worship the Creator God who made heaven and earth, while the third angel of (Revelation 14:9) warns against worshipping the beast or his image. Both the Mark of the Beast and the Seal of God take place in the "forehead," representing the place where you make your decisions. When you choose to worship the Creator God and declare your faithfulness to Him, you will be "marked" for protection by His angels during the time of trouble, which will come upon the earth prior to the return of Jesus Christ. It is like how the Israelites in Egypt applied blood on the lintels of their doors so that the destroying angel would pass over their homes.

Our choices will determine our destiny, but we are not alone in making choices that will impact our salvation. The Godhead has also made choices, as indicated below.

"For God so loved the world that He gave His only begotten Son, that whoever believes in Him should not perish but have everlasting life. For God did not send His Son into the world to condemn the world, but that the world through Him might be saved" (John 3:16).

"But God demonstrates His own love toward us, in that while we were still sinners, Christ died for us. Much more then, having now been justified by His blood, we shall be saved from wrath through Him" (Romans 5:8-9).

"Knowing that you were not redeemed with corruptible things, like silver or gold, from your aimless conduct received by tradition from your fathers, but with the precious blood of Christ, as of a lamb without blemish and without spot. He indeed was foreordained before the foundation of the world but was manifest in these last times for you who through Him believe in God, who raised Him from the dead and gave Him glory, so that your faith and hope are in God" (1 Peter 1:18-21).

"But we are bound to give thanks to God always for you, brethren beloved by the Lord, because God from the beginning chose you for salvation through sanctification by the Spirit and belief in the truth, to which He called you by our gospel, for the obtaining of the glory of our Lord Jesus Christ" (2 Thessalonians 2:13-14).

This Scripture confirms that it is the intention of the Godhead for all of us to be saved, and the mechanism for salvation has been made clear. We are to be sanctified (set apart) by the Holy Spirit and by our belief in the truth, which also sanctifies us. "Sanctify them by Your truth. Your word is truth" (John 17:17).

Summary

That concludes my open-source research into the Seal of God and the Mark of the Beast. I encourage you to undertake your own study and seek the guidance of the Spirit of God in arriving at the right conclusion, as the outcome will be crucial to your eternal destiny.

Revelation 14 provides a clear warning about whom to worship and the consequences of making the wrong choice. One path leads to eternal life, while the other leads to eternal death. This might sound frightening, but it doesn't have to be. Walk humbly with God, and He will guide you every step of the way.

To my Sunday-keeping readers, this is not meant to be a personal attack or criticism. It is about personal conviction. I urge believers of all persuasions to challenge the status quo and seek God's directives when it comes to how you worship Him. This is not about what your church believes; it is about you and your choices. Your church cannot save you, no matter how much truth it claims to have. Your priest or pastor cannot save you – some of them are openly robbing you in the name of Jesus for their own gratification. You do not need to give God anything (apart from your heart) for Him to bless you. Exercise and strengthen your faith daily because it will be tested beyond anything you are currently experiencing.

The Elephant in the Room

The euphemism "elephant in the room" refers to an obvious problem or issue that everyone is aware of but deliberately avoids discussing. This phrase is used to describe a situation where there is a significant and glaring problem or issue that is being ignored, often because it is uncomfortable or embarrassing to talk about.

"That said, if you currently worship on Sunday and that day becomes mandated and enforced, you might feel there is no choice to make, as you would simply continue following the tradition you and generations of your family have always practised—worshipping on Sunday.

However, the Mark of the Beast represents far more than an enforced day of worship; it signifies loyalty to human authority over God's commandments. In the end, there will be only two groups of people: those who remain faithful to God's original plan for His sacred day of worship and those who align themselves with the apostate regime.

However, if someone has always worshipped on Sunday without knowledge of the Sabbath truth, they are not held accountable in the same way as someone who knowingly rejects the Sabbath." "To him who knows to do good and does not do it, to him it is sin" (James 4:17).

Those most impacted by these draconian laws will be anyone who opposes the regime, who "love not their lives" and continue to uphold the unchangeable Ten Commandments of God, with the Saturday Sabbath at its heart. I must conclude that the Seventh-day Adventist Church and its members should be on high alert even now, because:

"The dragon (Satan) was enraged with the woman (God's church), and he went to make war with the rest of her offspring, who keep the commandments of God and have the testimony of Jesus Christ" (Revelation 12:17).

This issue of the Mark of the Beast is evidence that the Seventh-day Adventist Church is God's remnant church and the one that will incur the wrath of the dragon. While I acknowledge that there are other Sabbath-keeping churches, only one meets all the criteria of Revelation 12:17.

In recent times, there has been an increasing clamour to label the Seventh-day Adventist Church as a cult. However, the devil does not waste his time fighting against a cult. Proponents of this classification often point to some of our unique beliefs, such as the investigative judgment, to support their claim. This is because they misunderstand the concept. The pre-advent judgment is God allowing you and me to co-operate with Him to develop characters fit for heaven. It's about the confession of sins and daily reconciliation. God does not arbitrarily choose who will be saved; instead, He gives that privilege to us through the investigative judgment. What is far more problematic, and yet widely held by many Christians, is the belief that a loving God could simultaneously reside in one place while His unfaithful followers are tormented in eternal hellfire. Those who hold to this idea may struggle to reconcile such a notion with God's love, yet in doing so, they assume a position higher than God, whose ways and thoughts surpass ours. As the Lord says:

> "For My thoughts are not your thoughts,
> Nor are your ways My ways," says the Lord.
> "For as the heavens are higher than the earth,
> So are My ways higher than your ways,
> And My thoughts than your thoughts" (Isaiah 55:8-9).

Part of the criteria for consciously receiving the Mark of the Beast is that you will know the truth about the Seventh-day Sabbath, and that can only mean one thing—many will switch allegiance to preserve their freedom. The moment you make that decision, it will be a defining, light-bulb moment—one where you consciously choose to deny God to save your soul. The irony is that the opposite will be true: "For whoever desires to save his life will lose it, but whoever loses his life for My sake will find it" (Matthew 16:25). Here is the contrast to that: "And they overcame him by the blood of the Lamb and by the word of their testimony, and they did not love their lives to the death" (Revelation 12:11).

Victory Over the Beast and His Image

There's good news for those who choose to remain loyal to Christ in the great controversy with Satan. John, the writer of Revelation, declared: "I saw something like a sea of glass mingled with fire, and those who have the victory over the beast, over his image and over his mark and over the number of his name, standing on the sea of glass, having harps of God" (Revelation 15:2). This means that it wasn't just the Beast himself that was vanquished but everyone and everything that enabled him. The phrase "Image of the Beast" is interesting because it takes us back to creation when humankind was made in the "Image of God." It's the same word, but do they carry the same meaning, and was the context the same? Let's examine the image of the vanquished first.

The Image of the Beast

The Image of the Beast is a replica or representation of the Beast's authority and its system of worship. It symbolises a union of religious and political power that mirrors the original Beast, enforcing allegiance and persecuting dissenters: "And he deceives those who dwell on the earth by those signs which he was granted to do in the sight of the Beast, telling those who dwell on the earth to make an image to the Beast who was wounded by the sword and lived. He was granted power to give breath to the Image of the Beast, that the Image of the Beast should both speak and cause as many as would not worship the Image of the Beast to be killed" (Revelation 13:14-15). "He" refers to the second beast, also called the False Prophet, who "speaks like a dragon." The False Prophet works in conjunction with the first Beast to deceive the inhabitants of the earth. This power promotes worship of itself instead of God, coercing individuals to conform and threatening those who remain faithful to God.

The Bible repeatedly warns against worshipping the Beast or its Image (Revelation 14:9-11). Faithful followers of Christ are called to remain steadfast in their allegiance to God's commandments, even in the face of persecution or coercion. The Beast in Revelation is not directly Satan but is closely associated with him. The Beast represents earthly powers and systems under Satan's influence: "So the great dragon was cast out, that serpent of old, called the Devil and Satan, who deceives the whole world" (Revelation 12:9). Satan is explicitly identified as the dragon, the ultimate source of deception and rebellion against God. The First Beast (Revelation 13:1-10): The first Beast rises from the sea and represents a powerful political or religious system that opposes God. It derives its authority from the dragon (Satan): "The dragon gave him his power, his throne, and great authority" (Revelation 13:2). This Beast works as a tool of Satan to enforce his agenda on earth. The Second Beast: The second Beast arises from the earth and is often referred to as the False Prophet. It supports the first Beast, performing signs and enforcing worship of the first Beast's Image.

While the Beast is not Satan himself, it is a symbolic representation of systems and powers influenced by Satan. The dragon (Satan) operates through these entities to deceive and control humanity.

Mankind in the Image of God

"Then God said, 'Let Us make man in Our image, according to Our likeness; let them have dominion over the fish of the sea, over the birds of the air, and over the cattle, over all the earth and over every creeping thing that creeps on the earth.' So God created man in His own image; in the image of God He created him; male and female He created them" (Genesis 1:26–27). Humans were created to reflect God's moral, spiritual, and intellectual attributes, such as love, creativity, reasoning, and the capacity for relationships. This doesn't mean physical likeness (as God is Spirit – John 4:24) but a reflection of His character. Being made in God's Image includes dominion and stewardship over creation, acting as His representatives on Earth. The original Hebrew word for "image" in Genesis means resemblance, shadow, or representation. Whilst the Image of God includes dominion, stewardship, and being God's representatives on earth, the "Image of the Beast" represents false authority, forced worship, control, and rebellion against God. The Greek word for "image" in Revelation means likeness, representation, or figure. It is the same term used in the New Testament to describe humans being in the Image of God (e.g., Colossians 1:15), but the context determine its meaning. While the words for "image" are similar, their meanings differ based on context and source. Being made in God's Image reflects a divine calling and identity, while the Image of the Beast represents rebellion and allegiance to false authority. Mankind's purpose is to remain aligned with the Image of God, rejecting the deceptive pull of the Beast's counterfeit image.

Victory in Jesus

Evidence suggests that those who gained victory demonstrated unwavering faith in God, spiritual perseverance, and reliance on the redemptive work of Jesus Christ. They resisted the oppressive and deceptive powers of the Antichrist (the Beast) and his system of idolatry and rebellion against God. Their victory was not achieved through physical might but through spiritual faithfulness and reliance on God's power. The ultimate source of their victory is the Lamb, Jesus Christ. Revelation consistently emphasises that triumph comes through the blood of the Lamb (Revelation 12:11) and the word of their testimony. Their victory is celebrated in heaven, showing that their endurance on earth leads to eternal reward and glory. Finally, the victorious sing the "song of Moses" and the "song of the Lamb," praising God for His great and marvellous works, His justice, and His truth. This victory encourages us to stand firm in our faith, trusting in God's ultimate plan and power.

Chapter 14

Worship in Heaven

We can expect wholesale changes when Jesus comes again, and we begin to live with Him in the kingdom of glory when: "Mortal will have put on immortality" (1 Corinthians 15:53). Let us consider the building where worship will take place. "Heaven is My throne, and earth is My footstool. Where is the house that you will build Me? And where is the place of My rest?" (Isaiah 66:1). There is no building that can contain God, let alone all His worshipping creation. But we do read of worshippers coming before the Lord on His Holy Mountain in the new Jerusalem (Hebrews 12:22), and the services will not have a time limit. There will be no sermons as we know them today. Because sin and sinners will be no more, there is no need to preach the Word to convince anyone. No spectators passively watching; no chance to fall asleep; no appeals for funds to enrich pastors; no debates over dress codes; and no churches divided by nationality, tribe, or denomination. Come to think of it, if these activities won't exist in heaven, why not abandon them now? The examples that we see of heavenly worship convey a sense of unity of mind and purpose. And because we will be engaged in this throughout eternity, the closer we can get to heavenly worship in our services today, the better our experiences will be.

"'Eye has not seen, nor ear heard, nor have entered into the heart of man, the things which God has prepared for those who love Him.' But God has revealed them to us through His Spirit. For the Spirit searches all things, yes, the deep things of God" (1 Corinthians 2:9, 10). We can summarise worship in heaven—the new earth—as follows.

1. Preview of Heaven: The number of things that we experience today that will make it to the new earth, is very few, but God has given us a preview of certain eternal things.

    (a) Music and singing—According to the psalmist, David, we should: "Make a joyful shout to the Lord, all you lands, serve the Lord with gladness; come before His presence with singing. Know that the Lord, He is God; It is He who has made us, and not we ourselves, we are His people and the sheep of His pasture" (Psalm 100:1–3). In heaven, the Redeemed are pictured standing before the throne on the sea of glass with harps and, "They sing the song of Moses, the servant of God, and the song of the Lamb, saying: "Great and marvellous are Your works, Lord God Almighty! Just and true are Your ways, O King of the saints! Who shall not fear You, O Lord, and glorify Your name? For You alone are holy. For all nations shall come and worship before You, For Your judgments have been manifested" (Revelation 15:2–4).

    (b) The Sabbath—Since the beginning of human time, the Sabbath has revealed the dominion and sovereignty of the Creator-God. It started in the Garden of Eden and God enshrined it in the Ten Commandments on Sinai. It will continue throughout the ceaseless ages of eternity. "'And it shall come to pass that from one New Moon to another, and from one Sabbath to another, all flesh shall come to worship before Me,' says the Lord" (Isaiah 66:23).

    (c) Worship—Jesus told the Samaritan woman that "The hour is coming, and now is, when the true worshipers will worship the Father in spirit and truth; for the Father is seeking such to worship Him. God is Spirit, and those who worship Him must worship in spirit and truth" (John 4:23, 24). In heaven, we read how the twenty-four elders, "Fall down before Him who sits on the throne and worship Him who lives forever and ever, and cast their crowns before the throne, saying: 'You are worthy, O Lord, to receive glory and honour and power; for You created all things, and by Your will they exist and were created'" (Revelation 4:10, 11).

2. Worship God only: In a heavenly vision, the Apostle John fell at the feet of the heavenly messenger and started to worship him. But the messenger said, "See that you do not do that! I am your fellow servant, and of your brethren who have the testimony of Jesus. Worship God!" (Revelation 19:10).

3. Worship is responsive: When the achievements of God, or his mercy comes to mind, it prompts worship. "Then the seventh angel sounded: And there were loud voices in heaven, saying, 'The kingdoms of this world have become the kingdoms of our Lord and of His Christ, and He shall reign forever and ever!' And the twenty-four elders who sat before God on their thrones fell on their faces and worshiped God, saying: 'We give You thanks, O Lord God Almighty, the One who is and who was and who is to come, because You have taken Your great power and reigned'" (Revelation 11:15–17).

Here's another example: "Whenever the living creatures give glory and honour and thanks to Him who sits on the throne, who lives forever and ever, the twenty-four elders fall down before Him who sits on the throne and worship Him who lives forever and ever, and cast their crowns before the throne, saying: 'You are worthy, O Lord, to receive glory and honour and power; for You created all things, and by Your will they exist and were created'" (Revelation 4:9–11).

4. Worship is perpetual: Those who minister before the Lord are always engaged in worship. "The four living creatures, each having six wings, were full of eyes around and within. And they do not rest day or night, saying: 'Holy, holy, holy, Lord God Almighty, who was and is and is to come!'" (Revelation 4:8).

5. Worship is inclusive: We are not just speaking of the redeemed from the earth, but all the other unfallen worlds will come before the Lord on Sabbaths. "And every creature which is in heaven and on the earth and under the earth and such as are in the sea, and all that are in them, I heard saying: 'Blessing and honour and glory and power be to Him who sits on the throne, and to the Lamb, forever and ever!'" (Revelation 5:13). "'And it shall come to pass that from one New Moon to another, and from one Sabbath to another, all flesh shall come to worship before Me,' says the Lord" (Isaiah 66:23).

6. Worship glorifies God: "After these things I heard a loud voice of a great multitude in heaven, saying, 'Alleluia! Salvation and glory and honour and power belong to the Lord our God'" (Revelation 19:1).

7. Worship is celebratory: "Now when He had taken the scroll, the four living creatures and the twenty-four elders fell down before the Lamb, each having a harp, and golden bowls full of incense, which are the prayers of the saints. And they sang a new song,

saying: 'You are worthy to take the scroll, and to open its seals;
For You were slain, and have redeemed us to God by Your blood,
out of every tribe and tongue and people and nation, and have
made us kings and priests to our God; and we shall reign on the
earth.' Then I looked, and I heard the voice of many angels around
the throne, the living creatures, and the elders; and the number
of them was ten thousand times ten thousand, and thousands of
thousands, saying with a loud voice: 'Worthy is the Lamb who was
slain to receive power and riches and wisdom, and strength and
honour and glory and blessing!'" (Revelation 5:8–12).

Conclusion

To avoid any misunderstanding, let me clarify: worshipping on Sunday at present does not mean that you have the Mark of the Beast. Even when Sunday is enforced as a universal day of worship, the day itself will not be the defining characteristic. Those who receive the Mark will be individuals who, despite knowing the truth about the biblical Sabbath, choose to worship on Sunday instead of Saturday for the sake of self-preservation. They will also support this rebellious system through their actions and resources (symbolised by the mark on their hand).

This decision will not be trivial, as non-compliance will result in being unable to buy or sell, potentially losing employment, and facing betrayal even by family members. It is in this context that your faith will be tested to its absolute limit.

The Mark of the Beast and the Seal of God are both indicative of the choices you will make regarding whom you will worship – they are not physical marks on your forehead or forearm. Think of them in the same light as the phrase, "The mark of a man" (or woman), which refers to the combination of virtues and behaviours that define a person's character and ethical standing in society. It represents what a person stands for, their likes and dislikes, and how individuals conduct themselves and interact with others, highlighting qualities that are respected and valued.

So, what are the characteristics of the beast; what does he stand for? He has seven heads, and ten horns suggesting complex authority and power, possibly symbolising a coalition of kingdoms or powers aligned with it. The horns with crowns imply political authority. He claims divine authority, promoting teachings or practices that dishonour

God. He demands worship, indicating a global religious influence. He actively opposes God's faithful, seeking to suppress their worship and allegiance to God. The Mark of the Beast represents allegiance to a system that replaces God's authority with human traditions and laws.

The first angel of (Revelation 14:6) encourages us to worship the Creator-God who made heaven and earth, while the third angel of (Revelation 14:9) warns against worshipping the beast or his image. Both the Mark of the Beast and the Seal of God occur in the place where you make your decisions (your forehead or frontal lobes). When you choose to worship the Creator-God and declare your faithfulness to Him, you will be 'sealed' for protection by His angels during the time of trouble, which will come upon the earth prior to the return of Jesus Christ. It is like how the Israelites in Egypt applied blood on the lintels of their doors so that the destroying angel would pass over their homes.

Our choices will determine our destiny, but we are not alone in making choices that will impact our salvation. The Godhead has also made choices: "For God so loved the world that He gave His only begotten Son, that whoever believes in Him should not perish but have everlasting life. For God did not send His Son into the world to condemn the world, but that the world through Him might be saved" (John 3:16).

"But God demonstrates His own love toward us, in that while we were still sinners, Christ died for us. Much more then, having now been justified by His blood, we shall be saved from wrath through Him" (Romans 5:8-9).

"Knowing that you were not redeemed with corruptible things, like silver or gold, from your aimless conduct received by tradition from your fathers, but with the precious blood of Christ, as of a lamb without blemish and without spot. He indeed was foreordained before the foundation of the world but was manifest in these last times for you who through Him believe in God, who raised Him from the dead and gave Him glory, so that your faith and hope are in God" (1 Peter 1:18-21).

"But we are bound to give thanks to God always for you, brethren beloved by the Lord, because God from the beginning chose you for salvation through sanctification by the Spirit and belief in the truth, to which He called you by our gospel, for the obtaining of the glory of our Lord Jesus Christ" (2 Thessalonians 2:13-14).

This Scripture confirms that it is the intention of the Godhead for all of us to be saved, and the mechanism for salvation has been made clear. We are to be sanctified (set apart) by the Holy Spirit and by our belief in the truth: "Sanctify them by Your truth. Your word is truth" (John 17:17).

Summary

I hope you have been able to discern the facts and arrive at the same conclusion I have about the Mark of the Beast and the Seal of God. The ongoing conflict between Satan and Jesus Christ will continue until the Lord returns, so this is the time to make your decision.

We know the devil is a master of counterfeiting, creating substitutes for what he does not possess. God has ordained the Saturday Sabbath, while the devil seeks to enforce Sunday in opposition. One path of worship leads to death, and the other to life—choose life.

Exercise your faith daily because, if time shall last, it will be tested beyond anything you are currently experiencing. Do not be fearful of the time of trouble because: "At that time Michael (Jesus Christ) shall stand up, the great prince who stands watch over the sons of your people; and there shall be a time of trouble, such as never was since there was a nation, even to that time. And at that time your people shall be delivered, every one who is found written in the book" (Daniel 12:1). How do you get your name in heaven's book? Accept Jesus Christ as your Lord and Saviour.

God willing, I will see you in the heavenly congregation.

Printed in the United States
by Baker & Taylor Publisher Services